Seeking Hidden
TREASURES

Discovering the Mystery of God

Mary R. Sumners

ISBN 979-8-88851-029-2 (Paperback)
ISBN 979-8-88851-030-8 (Digital)

Copyright © 2023 Mary R. Sumners
All rights reserved
First Edition

All rights reserved. No part of this publication may be reproduced, distributed, or transmitted in any form or by any means, including photocopying, recording, or other electronic or mechanical methods without the prior written permission of the publisher. For permission requests, solicit the publisher via the address below.

Covenant Books
11661 Hwy 707
Murrells Inlet, SC 29576
www.covenantbooks.com

Contents

- I. Introduction 1
- II. **Guidelines for Investigating** 4
- III. **Follow the Clues** 18
    - I Believe, but Help My Unbelief 24
    - A Pure Heart 28
    - Perception vs. Sight 32
    - Trust in the Lord 36
    - The Truth Shall Set You Free 40
    - Know the Season 47
    - Assumption and Presumption 52
    - Brood of Vipers 58
    - A Hearing Heart 64
    - Still the Noise 68
- IV. **Begin Anew** 80
    - Searching for Identity 81
    - A Time of Restoration 88
    - God Is Sovereign 93
    - God Is Our Keeper 99
    - The Bond 104
    - Arise and Shine 109
    - Sonship 114
- V. **Becoming** 121
    - My Declaration 124
    - Moving by the Voice of God 130
    - Faith for the Journey 131
    - Positioned My Heart 134
    - Appropriated Strength 135
    - Prayer and Community Support 138

    New Posture 139
    I Am Weak, but He Is Strong 143
    Lay It Down 146
    The Elephant in the Room 150
    Drive Away the Vultures 153
    Put on the Garment of Praise 157
    Walking through the Storm 158
    The Parables 164
    War Cry 169
    Functional Sonship Is Our True Identity 176
    Loving with a Whole Heart 179
    The Key of David 184
    Kingdom of God 188
    They Must Match 193

VI. Knitting Our Hearts Together 197
    Equipping the Saints 200
    A Teaching Dimension 205
    The Parable of the Fig Tree 207
    The Secret Place 211
    The Hiding Place 216
    The Parable of the Watchman in the Tower 220
    A New Heart 227

VII. Being 232
    A Dominant Spirit 233
    Keep the Door Shut 237
    The Groan 243
    Designing a New Humanity 247
    Building a Kingdom Civilization 252
    Overcoming 258
    Hope Anchors Our Soul 263
    The Heart Follows the Treasure 268
    Love for the Body of Christ 275

Pay It Forward 279

Introduction

I pray that your hearts may be encouraged, being knit together in love, and attaining to all riches of the full assurance of understanding, **to the knowledge of the** mystery of God, *both of the Father and of Christ, in whom are* **hidden all the treasures of wisdom and knowledge**.
—from Colossians 2:2–3

Heavenly Father, open our eyes to see, our ears to hear and our heart to understand! ***Blessed are those whose strength is in you; Who have set their hearts on a pilgrimage.***
—Psalm 84:5 (WEB)

<u>Journeying without a destination is wandering</u>. Forty years ago, I set my heart to journey to find the hidden treasures of wisdom and knowledge in the Father and in Christ. I didn't really understand at the time that that was what I was doing.

Let me tell you my story. I came to know Jesus as my Savior at age twelve. I married at age eighteen and moved to California. We tried a couple of churches but gave up looking for the right one. The next ten years, I was busy attending college, and then I graduated and had two children. My second child had a health issue, which drove me back to attend church looking for God's comfort, strength, and wisdom.

Two years later, at age thirty, I was diagnosed with a serious chronic autoimmune disease. My response to the doctor was from Romans 8:28:

> We know that **all things work together for good for those who love God**, to those who are called according to his purpose.

> I told the doctor, "**God will work this for good in my life.** I don't know how, but **I believe** that he will." That is the stance that I have taken for forty years, and God has been faithful to do just as his Word says. Each time I have had an occurrence of diminished health, felt sick from medications, was in and out of the hospital, and had several surgeries, I ran to God for more sight of him. It has strengthened my core and given me perseverance to continue to seek him.

> Then, **let us offer up a sacrifice of praise to God continually**, that is, the fruit of lips which make confession to his name. (Hebrews 13:15 WEB)

As I write this book, I am offering my journey to God as a sacrifice of praise. I thank God for guiding me through the last forty years, never leaving nor forsaking me, building me in the image of his Son, and transforming me by the renewing of my mind.

> Don't be conformed to this world, but **be transformed by the renewing of your mind**, so that you may prove what is the good, well-pleasing, and perfect will of God. (Romans 12:2 WEB)

Our heavenly Father is a God of redemption. I praise him with a grateful heart and offer to him the fruit of my journey. As I share my journey with you, I pray that your heart may be encouraged and knit together in love as you attain all riches of the full assurance of understanding **to the knowledge of the mystery of God.**

Guidelines for Investigating

If you are a mystery buff, then this is the book for you. Did someone say "mystery"? If so, then count me in! Who wouldn't want to know more about the mystery of God and seek out all the treasures of wisdom and knowledge?

That thought challenged me to inquire of God and ask him to **unveil** his mystery. This is an account of that journey.

As we travel together, I will lead you through the process of investigation:

- Read Scriptures—the journey begins in seed form with the speaking of God
- Make a declaration of faith in alignment with the Scriptures—to plant the seed in your heart
- Look at **green clues** to answer question 1—seeing
- Look at **blue clues** to answer question 2—hearing
- Enter **red search word** to find your treasure.
- Give thanks and worship to God in prayer.
- Ask to receive your treasure, and place it in the treasure chest of your heart.

- How has it changed your <u>understanding? Journal your answer.</u>

God always begins with a seed. In order to plant the seed, you will find a **declaration of truth**, which will unfold in meaning as you grow and mature in your thinking. So Do Not despise small beginnings.

A seed—just a seed. What will it be?

The clues for **sight of the character and nature of God** are highlighted in **Green**.

This is a journey leading you to the full assurance of understanding the *mystery of God*. As you journey from clue to clue, **principle** to principle, you are **building a structure**. The "blueprint" is pulled from the invisible realm into the visible. So the principles are highlighted in **Blue**.

The Holy Spirit is your guide. The spirit of Christ is ascending, always ascending in you and you into him as your spiritual eyes are opened to see and hear more clearly. As you ascend in your journey, you will find a **key word** in **Red** <u>to enter the search box</u> of the Bible app. After your time of inquiry, you will find a **Red Box** <u>to record the treasure you discovered</u>. You may use a Bible program or app for acceleration and magnification. Do not take short cuts, or it will abort the process.

1. "Eat what is on your plate." That means to gain knowledge and understanding by proceeding one clue, one principle at a time. Taste it, chew it, and digest it before moving to the next clue. It is spiritual food. Jesus said, "I am true food." Take some time to **inquire** of God with a question, and listen for his answer.
2. Do not journey alone. It requires the synergy of collaboration to gain a more complete picture of the structure you are building. You will discover along the way what I mean when I say "structure."

The process of investigation

Sherlock Holmes, a fictional nineteenth-century sleuth from the pages of the books written by Arthur Conan Doyle has become an icon for solving mysteries using deductive reasoning. He is often portrayed at the scene of the crime with his magnifying glass in his hand as he scans the room, looking for clues. Our process will be similar.

The book of Proverbs speaks much about the wise man versus the foolish man. The mind of a logical man seeks knowledge through the five senses of sight, hearing, touch, taste, and smell and is often led astray in his thinking. It becomes man's perception of the rightness of life.

The fear of the Lord is the beginning of knowledge; **fools despise wisdom and instruction**.

You are seeking treasures of wisdom and knowledge of a spiritual nature discerned through the guidance of the Holy Spirit.

God gives **instructions** as to how to find wisdom.

> *My son, if you will **receive my words**, and **lay up my commandments with you**; so as to **incline you ear to wisdom**, and **apply your heart to understanding**; yes, if you **cry after discernment**, and **lift up you voice for understanding**; If you **seek her as silver**, and **search for her as for hid treasures**: Then you shall understand the fear of Jehovah, and find the knowledge of God. For the Lord gives wisdom.*
> (Proverbs 2:1–6)

To examine the mind of God more clearly, you will need a **magnifying glass** in the form of a Bible app. If you are not already using one, find a simple one to install on your mobile phone, tablet, and/or computer such as Bible Gateway.

You will use the app to examine the clue more closely. Enter the word into the search box to magnify the meaning by searching for this same word in other verses. As the Holy Spirit leads, you may want to extend your inquiry into a topical Bible dictionary to amplify the meaning of the clue. You are looking for that "aha" moment when you hear the small still voice of the Holy Spirit and gain sight. This is where Sherlock Holmes would say **"the game is afoot"**—meaning the search has begun. You will be searching to hear a word from God that changes the way you think. This is called a <u>transaction</u>. You have given him a declaration—in exchange, he will give you illumination. This is the renewing of your mind.

Partnership

Sherlock had a partner, Dr. Watson, who accompanied him as he investigated. I am asking you, **"Will you be my Watson?"** Will you walk by my side as we seek to discover the knowledge of the mystery of God together? As we walk together, we will also partner with God to lead us.

First, we will take the stance of a child so we do not begin the journey in the error of presumption or assumption.

> *Most assuredly I tell you,* **unless you turn, and become as little children, you will in no way enter into the Kingdom of Heaven.** *Whoever therefore* **<u>humbles himself as this little child</u>***, the same is the greatest in the Kingdom of Heaven.* (Matthew 18:3–4 WEB)

Praise and worship

<u>Sight of God activates worship</u>. Before we begin to investigate each clue, we will start with an attitude of thanksgiving and

make a declaration of faith. We are seeking hidden treasures in the Bible, the written word of God.

We are beginning with **Colossians 2:2–3:**

> *That their hearts may be comforted, they being knit together in love, and gaining all riches of the full assurance of understanding, that they may know the* mystery of God, *both of the Father and of Christ in whom are all the treasures of wisdom and knowledge hidden.*

Father, we lift our voice to you in thanksgiving and prayer:

Thank you, God, that you want to comfort our hearts and knit our hearts together in love. Thank you that you want to give us understanding and knowledge of the hidden treasures of wisdom. You are a loving Father, an all-knowing God in whom all the treasures exist.

Lead us, Lord, as we search. Open our blind eyes to **see**, open our deaf ears to **hear**, and give us a hearing heart to **understand** your nature and your ways. Lead us by your voice so that we may follow you.

You will move mountains

On my sixteen-year-old granddaughter's last day of camp, her counselor gave her a letter of appreciation for her participation and leadership. Her counselor's parting word was **"You will move mountains."** I picked her up from camp and asked her all about her adventure. After she had slept for about fifteen hours or close to it, we talked more. Then she asked me, "What was God's purpose in me receiving that word?"

Let's first hear my granddaughter's account of camp:

> This summer I enrolled in a Leaders in Training (LIT) two-week program at a YMCA summer camp. I worked behind the scenes in organizing and leading activities for children whose parents were part of the Wounded Warrior Project. It was an honor to serve the children of a military family, knowing every child I interacted with had one parent who was injured or killed during service. However, a crucial element of becoming a leader is discovering oneself, and my fellow LITs did seminars every morning to learn about ourselves. One of the first of these seminars was a talk to discover our purpose.
>
> One of our counselors, Dean, began by asking our group, "How many of you own an Apple product?" and almost every one of us raised our hands. Secondly, he asked, "How many of you own a Dell product?" and 2 people raised their hands. Dean asked us why we thought there was such a drastic change in the popularity of the company. Many of us believed it stemmed from the simplicity of Apple's products, how easy they are to use, but found out that was not a driving force. Dean drew a diagram for us, with an outer circle, labeled 'what', and slightly smaller circle within it, labeled 'how', and finally a center ring, labeled 'why'.
>
> We were asked, "Is it the 'what' resources that Apple has available to them in comparison to Dell, is it the metals or glass, the level of technology available to making products in

either company? I agreed with the group that it was not the 'what', or the physical means of doing something. Then we were asked, "Is it the how" the thinking behind a product, or the means of carrying it out? Does Apple have a better production line or supply than Dell, and is that the reason for their worldwide success?" I thought that it might be a minor factor, but that is not the reason behind the success of Apple relative to Dell. Finally, Dean explained, "The reason behind Apple's success and popularity relative to Dell is their 'why'. Apple's purpose is to revolutionize technology as we know it, to constantly strive for global connection through a new means of communication and technology. Apple's purpose and drive keeps them at the top.

"I invite you all to find your why, your purpose, what drives you every day. Start by asking what you like to do, what you enjoy in life, then continue to ask yourself why you like to do that, why do you find happiness in that one thing?" Dean told us.

As he explained how to find our purpose, I looked around me and found my peers discovering themselves. I found myself witnessing people whose purpose was to care, to include others, to help, to serve others. I found my 'why', my purpose as well. I believe that every decision we make, positive or negative, has reasoning behind it, an inspiration of sorts. If everyone made it their goal to inspire one other person to improve, to make a beneficial decision, think of how much better society would be. I decided that my purpose is to be an inspiration, to be a role model, because I aim to inspire in everything I do, even if I can inspire just one other person.

After finding our purpose, Dean asked us to look at the diagram again. He explained the importance of doing things with your purpose in mind, to work inside out, from why to how to what, instead of outside in. If you focus outside in, you close yourself off, leaving no room for growth and true purpose, because your physical 'what' is driving your spiritual 'why'. Yet if we grow inside out, we find ourselves building our lives with purpose and meaning, which will lead to true joy.

In building your life inside out, you open yourself to infinite opportunities and expansion. For example, when my friends would make a circle, facing inwards towards one another, we closed ourselves off to the campers around us. This also prevented any campers from joining us, showing the limits of building outside in. However, when I left the circle to go talk to a camper, I broke the circle and faced outwards, the same way we should build ourselves from the inside out. My counselors noticed this, how on multiple occasions, whether it be at the pool, the dance, or an activity, I would leave the circle to go talk to a camper. The other LITs would follow my example, and by my leadership, they no longer faced inward, but opened themselves to joy and new friendships with the children around us.

*****

Okay, let's talk about the what, how, why.

We will begin with the "**why**" and work from the inside out. Your center circle is your **core**—your beliefs, values, and attitudes. You have decided that your purpose is to inspire. The definition of inspire is

1. fill (someone) with the urge or ability to do or feel something, especially to do something creative.

> stimulate, motivate, encourage, influence, rouse, move, **stir**, energize, galvanize, incite
>
> Zerubbabel was commissioned by God to rebuild the temple, the house of God.
>
> Then Haggai, the Lord's messenger, spoke the Lord's message to the people, saying, "I am with you, says the Lord." So, the Lord **stirred up** the spirit of Zerubbabel the son of Shealtiel, governor of Judah, and the spirit of Joshua the son of Jehozadak, the high priest, and the spirit of all the remnant of the people; and they came and worked on the house of the Lord of hosts, their God. (**Haggai 1:13–14 NKJV**)
>
> synonyms: inspirational, encouraging, heartening, uplifting, stirring, **rousing**, stimulating, electrifying; moving, affecting, impassioned, influential
>
> **Wake up righteously**, (**arouse to the ways of the Lord**) and don't sin, for some have no knowledge of God. (**1 Corinthians 15:34 WEB**)

2. breathe in (air); inhale.

> Yahweh God formed man from the dust of the ground, and **breathed into his nostrils the breath of life; and man became a living soul. (Genesis 2:7 WEB)**

This was followed by a process of inquiry:
First, we searched the word *mountain*, which led us to Mark 11:23:

> *For most assuredly I tell you,* **whoever may tell this mountain**, *"<u>Be taken up</u> <u>and cast into the sea</u>," and <u>doesn't doubt in his heart, but believes</u> that what he says is happening; he shall have whatever he says.*

Then we looked at the preceding verse Mark 11:22 (WEB)**:**

> *Jesus answered them, "<u>Have <u>faith in God</u></u>."*

And Mark 11:24 (WEB):

> *Therefore I tell you,* **all things whatever you pray and ask for, believe that you have received them, and you shall have them.**

By faith she made a declaration: "I will move mountains." We continued with the process of seeking wisdom and knowledge to find the hidden treasure. I asked her to select a word to enter into the search box in the Bible app on my computer. She chose *believe*. We pulled up all the Scriptures with the word *believe*, and she selected John 12:36 (WEB):

> "While you have the light, **believe in the light, that you may become children of light**." Jesus said these things, and he departed and hid himself from them.

What is the nature of God (character) you see in this Scripture? He is the creator of life, a Father. God created man in his own image.

What is the principle that you hear? By believing in the light, his child will become a light in the likeness of his/her Father.

How do you move mountains? Think of the life of Jesus as a template. Look at his life. He is our pattern. Jesus was given capacity to act but not from his own strength. When God the Father anointed his son Jesus, he went from an ordinary carpenter to a supernatural being.

> *Jesus spoke to them, saying, "I am the light of the world. He who follows me will not walk in the darkness, but will have the light of life."*
> **(John 8:12 WEB)**

God gave him spiritual technology:

- **Understanding** to discern the intent of God
- **Counsel** to discover the plan and design in the mind of God
- **Might** with the power and capacity to act
- **Knowledge** with particular skills given by God to accomplish particular tasks
- A Positive **fear of the Lord**, which is the beginning of wisdom and restrains us from diverting from God's path and purpose

What is a mountain in your life?

It is any obstacle that hinders your journey to become a light in the likeness and image of your Father. The Bible calls a mountain to be every lofty thing raised up against the knowledge of God (2 Corinthians 10:5).

How has your new sight changed your understanding?
My granddaughter said, "My new understanding is that it is by his power, and in his timing, the mountain is removed. My part is to have faith in him, to ask and not doubt and believe that I have received."

<u>The Bible is God's instruction manual</u>.

> Every scripture inspired of God (is) also profitable for **teaching, for reproof, for correction, for instruction** which is in righteousness. That the man of God may be complete, furnished completely unto every good work. (2 Timothy 3:16–17 ASV)

If we don't read the Bible and spend some time inquiring of God, we do not know what to think or how to act.

<u>Jesus Christ is our pattern</u> of what a son looks like.

> And the Word became flesh, and dwelt among us (and we beheld his glory, glory as of the only begotten from the Father), full of grace and truth. (John 1:14 ASV)

<u>The Holy Spirit gives us the "rhema word" to guide us.</u>

> For the Holy Spirit shall teach you in that very hour what you ought to say. (Luke 12:12)

Worship and thanksgiving

Heavenly Father, we give you honor and glory that you are our creator. You are a loving father. You are the giver of life, and there is none like you. Thank you for your written word, for your Son Jesus who redeemed us to show us the way of righteousness, and for the Holy Spirit to guide us and give us counsel.

Thank you, Father, that you give us knowledge, wisdom, and power to move mountains in our lives so we may become a child of light shining in the darkness.

Let's get started moving mountains!

Watson, if you had a blueprint to build a house, where would you begin? You would first want to lay the foundation, right? That is what we are going to do in the next section.

We are going to practice applying the process to our thinking layer by layer as we look for treasures of wisdom and knowledge. If you have asked Jesus Christ into your heart to be your Lord and Savior, then you are born again in the spirit. Christ is in you.

> *Jesus answered him, "Most assuredly, I tell you,* **unless one is born anew, he can't see the Kingdom of God.**" (John 3:3 WEB)

When you make a declaration as to the truth of the Scripture, you are aligning your soul with your spirit. God, not my will be done but your will be done in my life. It is called "**perfected intent.**" You are declaring your intent to be conformed to the image of Christ.

> *How can a young man keep his way pure? By keeping it according to Your word.* (Psalm 119:9)

Your declaration would be to God: "I will keep my way pure by keeping it according to your Word." Then you have just declared your perfected intent to do so.

As we journey to discover the **mystery of God**, he will plant your feet on a pathway to maturity. It will take time and diligence, but the reward is well worth it.

The game is afoot.

Come along, Watson!

Grab your **"Sword of the Spirit"** (which is the word of God).

We are headed to the first mountain.

Follow the Clues

In this section, we will be learning to identify what a treasure of knowledge and wisdom looks like. We will practice this process multiple times as I give you clues using colored highlights.

Watson, look at the lead Scripture and then follow the clues.

> **Set your mind on the things that are above**, not on the things that are on the earth.
> (Colossians 3:2 WEB)

We are going toward the light. It reminds me of planting a seed into the ground which is darkness. As the seed dies into the ground, it begins a journey of growth and maturity, straining heavenward toward the light. The journey heavenward begins with dying to our will in order to seek his will for our life.

Jesus said to her, "I am the resurrection and the life. He who believes in Me, though he may die, he shall live. And whoever lives and believes in Me shall never die. Do you believe this?" She said to Him, "Yes, Lord, I believe that You are the Christ, the

Son of God, who is to come into the world." (John 11:25–27 NKJV)

Jesus prayed to his Father that we all be one in him and in the Father.

> *Not for these only do I pray, but for those also who believe in me through their word, **that they may all be one; even as you, Father, are in me, and I in you, that they also may be one in us;** that the world may **believe** that you sent me.* (John 17:20–21 WEB)

Make a declaration of faith (using the lead Scripture): God, I set my mind on things above. I strain heavenward and die to my will in order to seek your will for my life.

After you make a declaration (speaking it out loud to God), you may find a question or two to help guide you in your thinking.

- ❖ What do you believe?
- ❖ Is your heart open to hear truth and receive it?
- ❖ If not, ask God to show you what is holding you back, and lay it down. Die to it.

1. **What is the nature (character) of God that we see?**

God is the origin and giver of life. We see that the journey begins when God plants a seed in our heart. Our responsibility is to set our mind on things above and not things that are in the earth. We are to believe that God sent his Son into the world for resurrection to give us life.

2. **What is the kingdom principle that we hear?**

You must die to yourself in order to live in Christ.

The **key word to <u>enter into the search box</u>** of the Bible app is *believe*. Look at all the verses with the word *believe*. Ask God to lead you by the Holy Spirit to show you what he wants you to see. Look for a verse that jumps out and grabs your attention.

Your new sight may be fast, or it may take days to unfold the meaning as you meditate on it. Your Spirit is faster than your mind. The light travels from your heart, which is the gateway to your mind. When you gain new sight and understanding, this becomes your treasure.

Lay up for yourselves treasures in heaven**, where neither moth nor rust consume, and where thieves don't break through and steal; **for where your treasure is, there your heart will be also.(Matthew 6:20–21 WEB)

Enter *Believe* into the search box of your app.

I have done this for you. I chose the following verse—John 9:28—but I included the verse before and the verse after to assist us in understanding the context of the Scripture.

As you study the Scripture verse, you may want to use a commentary or topical dictionary to help you with some understanding.

*As Jesus passed by from there, two blind men followed him, calling out and saying, "Have mercy on us, son of David!" When he had come into the house, the blind men came to him. Jesus said to them, **"<u>Do you believe that I am able to do this</u>?"** They told him, "Yes, Lord." Then he touched their eyes, saying, "According to your* *faith be it done to you."* **(Matthew 9:27–29 WEB)**

> The two blind men **acknowledged their condition** and called out for help. They followed after Jesus, pursuing him. They called him son of David, which was a term used to describe the Messiah (Savior), thus acknowledging that they believed him to be the Messiah. **They humbled themselves to ask for mercy**.
>
> In return, Jesus asked them to make a confession of faith. He asked, <u>*"Do you* **believe** *that I am able to do this*</u>*?"* They said, *"Yes, Lord."*
>
> They believed in the truth of who Jesus said he was and believed in his power to do miracles. They came to him in submission to his will.
>
> In these verses is a pattern for faith:
>
> **Come to the Lord in humility, acknowledging that he is your Savior and your Lord. Pursue him. Ask him to open your blind eyes to see. Confess that he is able, and have faith to receive.**

Worship and thanksgiving prayer

Heavenly Father, thank you that **you are the giver of life**. There is no life outside of you. I believe that Christ is my Savior, and through him I receive your gift of eternal life. Thank you for sending your Son to earth **to die for me that I might be resurrected into life**. I pray to strain heavenward toward your light and set my mind on things above and not on things of the earth.

God, thank you for new sight to gain a better understanding of faith and believing in Jesus as my Savior and Lord. **I believe you are able to open my blind eyes to see the truth.**

Declare truth to receive your treasure to place in the treasure chest: God, you are able to open my blind eyes to see truth and change my thinking to be in alignment with your Word.

I receive **a mind set on things above**.

How has your new sight changed your understanding of God?
What do you hear God saying to you?

Journal

I Believe, but Help My Unbelief

Immediately the father of the child cried out with tears, **"I believe. Help my unbelief!"**
—Mark 9:24 (WEB)

A woman was once asked, "Are you the woman with the great faith?"

"No," she replied. "I am not the woman with the great faith, but I am the woman with a little faith in a great God."

Without faith it is impossible to be well pleasing to him, *for he who comes to God must believe that he exists, and that* **he is a rewarder of those who seek him.** (Hebrews 11:6 WEB)

The issue is finding God when we seek him. **Worship him in spirit and in truth. God is spirit**—the perfection of divine nature. God rewards us with increased **faith** when we worship him in truth and have sight of his divine nature and character. **Faith is activated by sight of God.**

Declaration of faith: Heavenly Father, as I gain more sight of you, I believe you will increase my faith so that I may be pleasing to you.

- ❖ Do you believe God exists as a spirit?
- ❖ Do you believe he rewards those who seek him?
- ❖ Do you desire to know more about the nature and character of God?

What is the nature of God that you see?
He is a rewarder to those who seek him.
What is the kingdom principle you hear?
Without faith, it is impossible to please God. Faith is activated by sight of God.

Enter *Faith* into search for inquiry.

> But if God so clothes the grass of the field, which today exists, and tomorrow is thrown into the oven, won't He much more clothe you, **you of little faith**? "Therefore, <u>don't be anxious</u>, saying, 'What will we eat?', 'What will we drink?' or, 'With what will we be clothed?' For the Gentiles seek after all these things, for your heavenly Father knows that you need all these things. But seek first God's Kingdom, and his righteousness; and all these things will be given to you as well." **(Matthew 6:30–33 WEB)**

> The issue here is not one of unbelief or not having faith, but it is lack of trust. God is described as clothing the grass of the field, which is the least of his creation when compared to you.
>
> So how much more will your heavenly Father make provision for your needs if you seek first his kingdom? The emphasis is on *seek*, to go in search of the truth. The kingdom is a spiritual dimension in which the Lord Jesus Christ reigns and rules as King.
>
> *We know that the Son of God has come, and <u>has given us an</u> <u>understanding</u>,* **that we know him who is true**, *and* **we are in him who is true**, *in his Son Jesus Christ. This is the true God, and eternal life.* **(1 John 5:20 WEB)**

Worship and thanksgiving prayer

God, you are the rewarder of those who seek you. I pray to seek first your kingdom and righteousness. **Thank you, God, that you will provide for my needs and I can trust you to do what you say you will do.** You cannot lie. You are Truth.

Declare truth to receive your treasure:

Sight of the one true God increases my faith. **O God, I ask for increased faith that I may be pleasing to you.**

How has your new sight changed your understanding of God?

What do you hear God saying to you?

Increased Faith

Journal

A Pure Heart

Blessed are the pure in heart, <u>for they shall see God</u>.
—Matthew 5:8 (WEB)

So, **a prerequisite to See God is to be pure in heart**—pure in mind, pure in motive, and pure in principles. Man looks on the outward appearance, but **God looks at our heart**.

How often do we go to God in prayer to ask him to fix something such as a relationship with a family member or friend, our finances, overcome depression, chronic health issues, etc., to make it right according to our desire? And the list goes on and on, or we go to God, seeking a blessing to be bestowed upon us. The conundrum for God to respond to these types of prayers is that me, myself, and I are at the center of our focus. How do you lead one upward when he/she is looking inward?

Jesus was the greatest servant that ever lived. Jesus said, "My food is to do the will of him who sent me and to finish his work."

> But **seek first God's Kingdom, and his <u>righteousness</u>**; and all these things will be given to you as well. (Matthew 6:33 WEB)

Remember, sight of a mighty, powerful, awesome, sovereign God and increased faith are related one to the other.

Declaration of faith: God, I will seek first your kingdom and your righteousness.

- ❖ What do you think it means to seek first God's kingdom and his righteousness?
- ❖ Knowing the God to whom you are praying will determine your stance before him.

What is the nature of God that you see?
God is pure. He is holy.
What is the kingdom principle you hear?
Seek God's kingdom first to live accurately in the truth of his ways, and he will meet our needs.
Enter *Heart* into search for inquiry.

> *Trust in the Lord, and do good; Dwell in the land, and feed on His faithfulness. Delight yourself also in the Lord, And He shall give you the desires of your heart.* **(Psalm 37:3–4 NKJV)**

> Delight in the character, will, and ways of God. Trust in him and do good, and he will be faithful to grant you the desire of your heart (those things for which you ask of him).
>
> The fact that you seek your pleasure in him will regulate your desires so that you will be "disposed" to ask only those things proper for him to grant, and the fact that you do find your joy in him will be a reason why he will grant your desires (Barnes Commentary).
>
> *This is the boldness which we have toward him, that, if we ask anything according to his will, he listens to us. And if we know that he listens to us, whatever we ask, we know that we have the petitions which we have asked of him.* (1 John 5:14–15 WEB)

Worship and thanksgiving prayer

God, you are pure, divine, holy, and righteous. There is no darkness in you. Thank you, God, that **I can trust you to give me the desires of my heart if I delight myself in your character, your will, and your ways. Thank you that I can be bold to ask.**

Declare truth to receive your treasure: Father, I choose to delight in you, and I ask you to **give me a pure heart so that I can see you accurately** to know your heart and your ways.

> A Pure Heart to See God

How has your new sight changed your understanding of God?

What do you hear God saying to you?

Journal

Perception vs. Sight

Thus says the **Lord who made the earth, the Lord who formed it to establish it,** *the Lord is His name,* **"Call to Me, and I will answer you, and show you great and mighty things, which you do not know."**

—Jeremiah 33:2–3 (NAS)

When God delivered the Israelites out of the land of Egypt, they did not know or understand that he would raise them up to be a mighty army. They found their identity in what they did every day. They saw themselves as "just brick makers."

After being delivered from Egypt, Moses sent twelve spies into the land of promise. Ten reported that the giants were too big for them to overtake the land, saying, "We were in our own sight as grasshoppers, and so we were in their sight."

But Caleb had sight of his God and said, "Let us go up at once and possess it, for we are well able to **overcome** it."

God later revealed to Jeremiah:

> **You are my battle axe** **and weapons of war**: and with you will I break in pieces the nations; and with you will I destroy kingdoms.

God says his purpose is against Babylon to destroy it. Babylon represents a society which worships false gods in rebellion against God. In the book of Revelation, Babylon is labeled as a mystery, the mother of the harlots and the abominations of the earth.

People are feeling unstable as our world sinks deeper into crisis, but we have a choice to perceive ourselves as "just a brick maker" or to see ourselves in truth as a mighty warrior, the battle axe of God.

Declaration of faith: God, I believe if I call to you that you will answer me and show me great and mighty things I

do not know. I believe I am your battle axe, and with me, you will break the nations of the world.

- ❖ Which one do you choose? Brick maker or battle axe?
- ❖ Do you want more sight of your true identity?

What is the nature of God that you see?

God is the Creator and sovereign over all. He created the earth and established everything in it.

What is the kingdom principle you hear?

If we call out to God, who has the power to open our eyes to reveal the invisible realm, he says he will show us great and mighty things.

Enter *Overcome* into search for inquiry.

> *For whatever is born of God overcomes the world. This is the victory that has **overcome** the world: your faith. Who is he who overcomes the world, but he who believes that Jesus is the Son of God?* **(1 John 5:4–5 WEB)**

> Our perception in the world is that we are weak, and the enemy is stronger. Our flesh is weak and easily tempted. However, Jesus said, *"In the world you have oppression; but cheer up! I have overcome the world"* (1 John 16:33).
>
> By his death on the cross, Jesus defeated the prince of this world. The victory is ours for the asking. Jesus revealed the true nature of the Spirit within us and the strength to overcome the world when we abide in him. Our existence on earth is not without trials and

> tribulations, but Jesus provides peace and refuge as we journey through them.

Worship and thanksgiving prayer

Father God, **you are the Creator of heaven and earth. You are Sovereign over all.** You alone have the right to define my identity. I thank you that **you have said that you will show me great and mighty things if I call out to you.**

Declare truth to receive your treasure: God, I am your battle axe. I call out to you to open my eyes and show me my **true identity**.

How has your new sight changed your understanding of God?
What do you hear God saying to you?

Journal

Trust in the Lord

I have put my trust in God. I will not be afraid. **What can man do to me?**

—Psalm 56:11 (WEB)

Trust is belief, hope, confidence, and reliance in God and Jesus Christ. It requires conviction and commitment. In the Old Testament, we find a long list of Bible heroes who trusted the nature of God and trusted in the ways of God: Noah, Abraham, Sarah, Isaac, Jacob, Joseph, and Moses, just to name a few.

Abel and Enoch are described as living by faith. Abraham "believed in the Lord," and the prophet Habakkuk taught that "The just shall live by his faith" (Habakkuk 2:4).

We have a choice of how we will respond when we are faced with bad news that will greatly affect our life. The news can destabilize us with fear, OR we can say "but God says." In the Psalms, David often pours out his heart as he describes his afflictions and his feeling of being overcome by his enemies, but his pattern for deliverance was to turn his thoughts around and declare the truth of his God:

- But God says he is my refuge and strength, a very present help in time of trouble. (Psalm 46:1)
- But God says to call upon him in the day of trouble and he will deliver me and I shall glorify him. (Psalm 50:15)
- But God says he is a strong tower; the righteous run to him and are safe. (Proverbs 18:10)
- But God says he is my hiding place and a shield to those who hope in his word. (Psalm 119:114)
- But God says he will never leave me nor forsake me. (Hebrews 13:5)

David **was continually running to God for deliverance**. *Trust in him at all times, you people. Pour out your heart before him. God is a refuge for us* (Psalm 62:8 WEB).

Declaration of faith: I put my trust in you, God, and I am not afraid of what man can do to me. God, I will pour out my heart to you and take refuge in you.

- ❖ Do you believe the report of the enemy?
  OR
- ❖ Do you believe God will deliver you from the enemy?

What is the nature of God that you see?
God is trustworthy.
What is the kingdom principle you hear?
I am able to pour out my heart to him, for he is my refuge.
Enter *Trust* into search for inquiry.

> *But I **trust** in your loving kindness. My heart rejoices in your salvation.* **(Psalm 13:5 WEB)**

I TRUST YOU

The Psalms talk about taking counsel from our soul and having sorrow in our heart every day as the enemy rejoices over us. Refuge is a shelter from that which threatens us from the outside and a sanctuary for us on the inside. It is a place where we can go with our thoughts and "still the noise" to have peace in our heart and mind.

***Trust** in the Lord with all your heart, and lean not on your own understanding; In all*

> *your ways acknowledge Him, And He shall direct your paths.* To acknowledge is to commit your way unto him. God promises that if we do this, he will direct our path. **(Proverbs 3:5–6 NKJV)**

Worship and thanksgiving prayer

God, you are trustworthy. You are my salvation. Thank you, God, **that I can pour out my heart to you, and you will give me shelter from the enemy** who seeks to destroy me. I commit my way to you and put my trust in you to make my path straight.

Declare Truth to receive your treasure:
God, you are **my shelter**, my hiding place. **I trust you.**

How has your new sight changed your understanding of God?
What do you hear God saying to you?

Journal

The Truth Shall Set You Free

If you abide in my word, you are truly my disciples; and you shall know the truth, and the truth shall set you free.
—John 8:31–32

To be free means to no longer be held captive by the sin that endangers our relationship with God. The enemy persists in trying to invade our thoughts in order to get us to act in a way contrary to kingdom life and to not be in alignment with the values and principles of God.

"Abide in the Word of Christ" means to remain in the Word and have the Word remain in you. Jesus said, "*I am the way, the truth, and the life. No one comes to the Father, except through me*" (John 14:6).

> *Though we walk in the flesh, we don't wage war according to the flesh; for the weapons of our warfare are not of the flesh, but mighty before God to the throwing down of strongholds,* **throwing down imaginations and every high thing that is exalted against the knowledge of God***, and bringing every thought into captivity to the obedience of* **Christ.** (2 Corinthians 10:3–5 WEB)

The enemy uses three areas to tempt us—the lust of the eye, the lust of the flesh, and the pride of life. It is plain to see the tactics of the enemy when he tempted Eve in the garden and again when he tempted Jesus in the wilderness following Jesus's baptism in the Jordan River.

> *By this we know that we remain in Him and He in us, because He has given us of his Spirit.* (1 John 4:13 WEB)

When I hear the enemy putting thoughts in my head, I take it captive by saying, "That is not my voice." I reject it and move on. We are bombarded in this fast-paced digital world with marketing, Facebook, Tik Tock challenges, imagery, competitive thinking, etc., resulting in confusion as to our true identity and value. The issue is to discern whether the thoughts are kingdom ways or Babylonian ways.

Babylon is a system in the world today. *Babel* means "confusion or mixture." Sometimes we say it is a half-truth. The enemy leads us to believe it is something good and twists the truth to pervert the meaning.

When my granddaughter was young, I saw the opportunity for a teachable moment and played a game with her. If we saw something on television or someone acting in a particular way, I would ask her, "Is that kingdom, or is that of the world?" And she would choose one or the other. When she was little, I made it easy for her to distinguish between the two. When she became a teenager and it was not so black and white but grey, it led to a discussion of her expressing her opinion with my rebuttal.

I will give you a few seemingly harmless examples:

It is the custom to celebrate Halloween on the eve before All Saint's Day. The first time my young granddaughter went trick or treating, she was going from house to house, saying, "Happy Halloween, Merry Christmas, and Happy Easter." She had no idea why she was dressing up and going to neighbors' houses for candy only to come home and have her mother sort through it and throw half of it away. In the US, we spend two billion dollars on candy every Halloween. We spend seven hundred thousand dollars over a five-year period on costumes for our pets (from *America Fact or Fiction* TV show). Why?

The early tradition for Thanksgiving Day in the colonies was a day of fasting by the Puritans to give thanks to the Lord. It is now a day of feasting. Christmas is supposed to be a day to celebrate God's gift to us of his Son but has been twisted to become a commercialized season of spending money.

I am even becoming annoyed with birthday cards **wishing** you a "happy birthday." First of all, what is a wish? There is no power in a wish, and "happy" is a worldly term not relevant in the kingdom of God. We are to have joy.

You may think I am being too harsh. This is not a comment to ridicule any person or business. Remember, we do not war against flesh and blood. Jesus rebuked the Pharisees once again by saying,

> ***You have made the commandment of God void because of your tradition.***
> (Matthew 15:6 WEB)

Do you do that?

When we journey through the book, you will come to see that we have been taught to worship false gods.

> **We do not fall from grace because we sin; we sin because we have restricted the flow of grace into our life.**

King David plotted to have Bathsheba's husband killed so he could take her as his wife. The Lord sent his prophet Nathan to rebuke, admonish David. Nathan told David a parable about a rich man who had taken from the poor man and sinned against him. Then Nathan declared to King David, "You are the man." When David understood the warning, he said to Nathan, "I have sinned against the Lord."

David was a worshipper who had a reverent fear of the Almighty God. **Repentance and worship will return us to an accurate alignment with kingdom values and principles and restore our relationship with God.**

Remember that the **fear of the Lord is the beginning of knowledge**; fools despise wisdom and instruction. If one does not have a reverent fear of the Lord, he has not even started to know the Lord (to have a relationship with Him). **Fear of the Lord is the True Foundation of Knowledge.**

Declaration of faith: God, I will abide in your Word so that I shall know the truth to set me free.

- Ask God to show you if there is a place in your life where the tradition of man is more important than honoring the ways of God.
- Are you quick to repent when you receive correction from the Lord?
- Do you worship him to restore your peace and stand among the wise?

What is the nature of God that you see?
God is a God of deliverance and the source of peace.
What is the kingdom principle you hear?
A repentant heart and an attitude of worship and thanksgiving will restore our relationship and communion with God.
Enter *Abide* into search for inquiry.

> The ear that hears the rebukes of life **will abide among the wise**. He who disdains instruction despises his own soul, but **he who heeds rebuke gets understanding. The fear of the Lord is the instruction of wisdom**, and before honor is humility. **(Proverbs 15:31–33 NKJV)**

SEEKING HIDDEN TREASURES

> There are three truths mentioned in the verses:
>
> 1. Have ears to hear words of wisdom spoken in rebuke by God.
> 2. Obey the counsel given, and you will get understanding.
> 3. Receive instruction from the Lord with humility, and live with honor.
>
> **Wisdom** is the spiritual impartation that <u>comes before action</u>. Impartation has to do with the giving and receiving of a dimension of the divine Spirit to sustain you in the work of his calling on your life.
>
> *Wisdom is the principal thing; therefore get wisdom. And in all your getting, get understanding.* (Proverbs 4:7 ASV)
>
> Simply said—abide (stand, remain) in the Word; hear, obey, get wisdom, get understanding, **and then act**.

Worship and thanksgiving prayer

Heavenly Father, **you are a wise God**. Thank you that you reprove us because you love us. Your desire is for us to look like your Son Jesus and to **know the truth that shall set us free from sin and death.**

Declare truth to receive your treasure: God, I choose to **abide in the truth, receive wisdom, and get understanding** to be set free from the lies and deceit of the enemy.

Set Free

> **Abide in the truth, receive wisdom, and get understanding**

How has your new sight changed your understanding of God?

What do you hear God saying to you?

Journal

Know the Season

When he (Jesus) drew near, he saw the city and wept over it...because you didn't know the time of your visitation.
—Luke 19:41, 44 (WEB)

God moves in the earth in times and seasons. It is imperative to know the time and season in which you live and exist. Just like Noah, we bring into reality now the things we see by faith in the future.
Faith looks forward.

> *Now faith is assurance of (things) hoped for, a conviction of things not seen.* (Hebrews 11:1 ASV)

When the temple in Jerusalem was destroyed in AD 70, the Israelites found themselves without a place to sacrifice, without a place to make offerings, and without a holy of holies for the priest to sprinkle blood on the mercy seat on the day of atonement. God moved on from a covenant of law to a covenant of grace.

The Jews that had not seen the day of their visitation remained in an old order, an old tradition that had no life. God was no longer in it. Jesus had fulfilled the Law, been raised from the dead and seated as our High Priest in heavenly places and God moved into a covenant of grace.

Remember, we are on a journey toward a destination. The season requires us to be appropriately dressed and equipped to follow God.

The ears of the spirit are in the heart, not in the head; they are in the heart.

> *The spirit of a man is the lamp of the Lord, searching all the inner depths of his heart.* (Proverbs 20:27 NKJV)

Declaration of faith: God, by faith I will build a present-day structure for a future event.

- ❖ Are you seeking to follow God with your head or your heart?
- ❖ Are you willing to incline your ear to wisdom, apply your heart to understanding, and cry out for discernment?

What is the nature of God that you see?
God is a God of order and sequence. He advances his purpose in the earth in times and seasons as we journey toward the finish.

What is the kingdom principle you hear?
Faith looks forward. By faith, we bring into reality now the things we see in the future.

Enter *Heart* into search for inquiry.

> *Then the Lord saw that the wickedness of man was great in the earth, and that every intent of the thoughts of his heart was only evil continually. And the Lord was sorry that He had made man on the earth, and He was grieved in His heart. So, the Lord said, "I will destroy man whom I have created from the face of the earth."* **(Genesis 6:5–7 NKJV)**

> But *Noah found grace (favor) in the eyes of the Lord.* (Genesis 6:8)
>
> The paternal God was greatly offended that mankind had chosen to reject his lov-

ing-kindness and "grieved in his heart," **alienated (separated) from his creation**; but Noah "walked with God," and God entered into a covenant with Noah to deliver him and his family from destruction. Noah is described as a "just man and perfect in his generation." Noah bore constant testimony against the unbelief and wickedness of that generation for 120 years while he built the ark.

Noah was not a perfect man, as we see later in his life, but was called perfect in his generation. Noah partnered with God to complete God's purpose in the earth in that time and season. Noah was faithful to hear and obey God in the midst of a hostile environment.

Worship and thanksgiving prayer

God, you are a God of order and sequence. Thank you for the faith to partner with you to build a structure now to be used later for your purpose in the earth.

Declare truth to receive your treasure.

Father, I cry out for **discernment to know your heart's desire and have the** perseverance to complete your purpose **in my generation.**

Discernment to Know God's Plan

SEEKING HIDDEN TREASURES | 49

How has your new sight changed your understanding of God?

What do you hear God saying to you?

Journal

Assumption and Presumption

***The mind of man plans his way, but** the Lord directs his steps*.
—Proverbs 16:9 (NAS)

If you formulate a way in your mind to make God's will your destination, then you may expect that he will direct your steps by his spirit and **grace**.

When someone asked me to define *grace*, I said, "That is not so simple." Some have said it is the undeserved love and favor of God. When I was younger, I was told it is **G**od's **R**iches **a**t **C**hrist's **E**xpense. If you google the meaning of *grace*, it may help, but it is lengthy.

So I asked God to explain it to me, and this is what I heard. Let's start with the fact that Christ is the head, and we (believers) are called the body of Christ. In the head is the brain, the control center.

Grace is the ability to function from the brain of Christ, to think like he would think, but that immediately sets up a conflict with our soul. If you were to say that you want something with all your heart and soul, you are saying, "I desire it, and by my will, I permit it to happen."

Our physical body has a brain which controls our body including the feeling of pleasure and comfort. If I am comforted by eating chocolate, then by my will, I permit myself to do it, and my brain will cooperate to go seek it and eat it.

If we desire to be like Christ, God gives us the grace to function from the brain of Christ, but our will has to submit to receive the grace and bypass the desires of our flesh. That is called dying to self.

Let this mind be in you which was also in Christ Jesus. (Philippians 2:5 NKJV)

He humbled Himself and became obedient to the point of death. (v. 8)

> **Grace is like an authorized hard wire connection transmitting data from the mind of Christ, bypassing our fleshly desires and fears and landing in our mind to deposit a treasure.**

We must beware of interpreting the Word to our own assumption and presuming we know what to do without waiting on the Lord to direct us and establish our steps. Beware if you are feeling compelled to act without waiting to hear the voice of God, or you may hear the Lord guiding you in a way that makes no sense to the logical mind and choose to ignore it by assuming that you are not hearing correctly.

> Pin up a sign in your mind that says,
> **I ONLY MOVE BY THE VOICE OF GOD.**

Without counsel purposes are disappointed; but in the multitude of counsellors they are established. (Proverbs 15:22 DAR)

Collaboration is partnering with other saints to seek the mind of God within the context of the season. We seek to align our sight with God's intentions and desires in order for his will to be revealed and executed. Collaboration creates momentum in our journey to the finish of God's purpose in the earth.

He gave some to be apostles; and some, prophets; and some, evangelists; and some, shepherds and teachers for the perfecting of the saints, to the work of serving, to the building up of the body of Christ; until we all attain to the unity of the faith, and of the knowledge of the Son of God, to a full grown man, to the measure of the stature of the fullness of Christ. (Ephesians 4:11 WEB)

Our God is a God of direction. *God has set some in the assembly: first apostles, second prophets, third teachers, then miracle workers, then gifts of healings, helps.* (1 Corinthians 12:28 WEB)

The apostle Paul said, "**You all are partakers with me of grace**." In submitting to the grace from God upon the apostle, you become a partaker of that same grace which was upon him.

Declaration of faith: God, I submit to the grace that flows from Jesus Christ to build me and direct my steps.

What is the nature of God that you see? God is an instructor to lead us in his ways.

What is the kingdom principle you hear?

It is the grace of God which instructs and leads us in his ways.

Enter *Grace* **into search for inquiry.**

From his fullness we all received grace upon grace. For the law was given through Moses. ***Grace*** *and truth came through Jesus Christ.* **(John 1:16–17 WEB)**

Grace is the undeserved love and favor of God. You cannot earn it.

God's grace frees us from slavery to <u>sin, guilt, and shame</u>. Grace enables us to live an abundant life in Christ.

The thief only comes to steal, kill, and destroy. I came that **they may have life and may have it abundantly**. **(John 10:10 WEB)**

Grace opens our blind eyes to see differently and persevere to make right choices. The apostle Paul walked in the grace of God and did not waver when faced with the opposition toward him in the earth. He looked upward to receive strength, wisdom, discernment, might, and understanding to complete God's purpose for his life just as we are to do also.

Worship and thanksgiving prayer

God, you are a good Father **who instructs** us in the ways of kingdom life. Thank you for the **grace and truth which came through Jesus Christ that I may have life and have it abundantly.**

Declare truth, and receive your treasure.

Grace is truth, wisdom, and understanding given to me through Jesus Christ. I receive an **abundance of grace**—the mind of Christ.

How has your new sight changed your understanding of God?

What do you hear God saying to you?

Journal

Brood of Vipers

The good man out of the good treasure of his heart brings out that which is good, and the evil man out of the evil treasure of his heart brings out that which is evil, for *out of the abundance of the heart, his mouth speaks.*
—Luke 6:45 (WEB)

Jesus called the Pharisees a generation of vipers, referring to them as the offspring of a poisonous snake. They had added additional laws to the 613 laws of Moses and thought themselves to be above sinners. They were self-righteous and prideful and often scolded by Jesus. Jesus's critique of the Pharisees was that they were legalistic and only concerned with the external appearance of keeping the Law rather than the inward spirit of the Law. The Pharisees were bitter and persistent enemies and sought to destroy Jesus's influence on the people.

God resists the proud, but gives grace to the humble. (James 4:6 NKJV)

And he (Jesus) spoke also a parable to them: Can a blind [man] lead a blind [man]? shall not both fall into the ditch. **The disciple is not above his teacher**, but every one that is perfected shall be as his teacher. (Luke 6:39 DBY)

The Pharisees represent a blind religious order leading others into the ditch. They had no sight to see that Jesus was the Son of God. They had appointed themselves to be the judge over the less-fortunate sinners.

For God has not sent his Son into the world that he may judge the world, but that **the world may be saved through him**. (John 3:17 DBY)

> Our **God is a God of redemption**. *There is therefore now no condemnation to them that are in Christ Jesus.* (Romans 8:1 ASV)

Satan is a deceiver and blinds unbelievers. He also is a slanderer and accuser of the saints. He is a liar.

> *Forget the former things. Begin anew. Behold I will do a new thing.* (Isaiah 43:19 DBY)

Declaration of faith: God, I believe you sent Jesus into the world to save me and that you will do a new thing in me.
What is the nature of God that you see?
God is redemptive. He saves us from destructive ways and restores us to right thinking and actions.
What is the kingdom principle you hear?
God resists the proud but gives grace to the humble. A man will speak forth from what is in his heart.
Enter *Judge* into search for inquiry.

> ***So let a man think of us as Christ's servants, and stewards of God's mysteries.*** *Here, moreover, it is required of stewards, that they be found faithful.* **(1 Corinthians 4:1–2 WEB)**

> *Therefore judge nothing before the time, until the Lord comes,* **who will both bring to light the hidden things of darkness, and reveal the counsels of the hearts.** *Then each man will get his praise from God.* **(1 Corinthians 4:5 WEB)**

> As a faithful servant, we steward, administer the resources of the mysteries of God. (You will learn how to do this as we journey.)
>
> *For the word of the cross is foolishness to those who are dying, but to us who are saved it is the power of God… Where is the wise? Where is the scribe? Where is the lawyer of this world? Hasn't God made foolish the wisdom of this world?* **(1 Corinthians 1:18, 20 WEB)**
>
> *Everyone therefore who <u>hears these words of mine</u>,* (the written word of Jesus Christ and rhema word of God) *<u>and does them</u>, <u>I will liken him to a wise man, who built his house on a rock</u>.* **(Matthew 7:24 WEB)**
>
> The opinions of the world are foolishness. We are not interested in what is politically correct or what the earth thinks or what natural reality tries to storm into our mind. The ways of unbelievers demonstrate foolishness disguised as wisdom.
>
> We only seek the divine architecture of God to build something that God wants.

Worship and thanksgiving prayer

God, **you are redemptive**. Thank you for the written words of Christ and your utterance to make us wise stewards.
  Declare truth, and receive your treasure.
  I **humble myself before you, God, and ask you** for **wisdom to build accurately**.

Wisdom to **Build**
Accurately

How has your new sight changed your understanding of God?

What do you hear God saying to you?

Journal

Journal continued:

A Hearing Heart

*Give therefore to thy servant an **understanding heart**, to judge thy people, to discern between good and bad; for who is able to judge this thy numerous people?*
—1 Kings 3:9 (DBY)

God came to King Solomon in a dream and said, "**Ask** what I shall give you." Solomon asked for a heart that hears and can discern, distinguish between good and bad.

> *Ask, and it shall be given to you. Seek, and ye shall find. Knock and it shall be opened to you. For every one that asks receives; and he that seeks finds; and to him that knocks it shall be opened.* (Matthew 7:7–8 DBY)

This verse assures us that a Christian who asks with a sincere heart will receive a truthful answer. Solomon praised God for his loving-kindness, acknowledged God's sovereignty to make him king, defined himself as a servant, and humbly referred to himself as a little child in need of a hearing heart to understand the ways of God.

> *Every good gift and every perfect gift comes down from above, from the Father of lights, with whom is no variation nor shadow of turning.* (James 1:17 DBY)

Jesus Christ is the "Light of the world," the dear Son of 'the Father of the lights.'"

Ask with a proper spirit, with humility, sincerity, and perseverance, knowing that

> **God is Sovereign and life is by design.**

> *And the word pleased the Lord, that Solomon had asked this thing.* (1 Kings 3:10 DBY)

Declaration of faith: Father God, I acknowledge your sovereignty over all creation. I am your servant and come to you as a little child in need of a hearing heart to understand your ways.

❖ What do you desire to ask from God?

What is the nature of God that you see?
God is sovereign.
What is the kingdom principle you hear?
Everyone who asks humbly with a sincere heart will receive an answer, and he who perseveres to seek and pursue God will be rewarded with sight, the ability to receive knowledge and wisdom.
Enter *Ask* into search for inquiry.

> *Now to him who is able to do exceedingly abundantly above all that we **ask** or think, according to the power that works in us.* **(Ephesians 3:20 WEB)**

> Because of God's love and grace to us, he is able and will "do exceedingly abundantly above all that we **ask** or think." Paul is praising and giving thanks and encouraging the saints to have hope for the future.
>
> His ways are not our ways. He is able to do beyond what we ask or think—a super abundance, an infinite abundance. This should increase our faith because it is not our ability

SEEKING HIDDEN TREASURES | 65

> but God's power through the Holy Spirit working within us.

Worship and thanksgiving prayer

You are my **sovereign Lord**. Thank you for giving me a hearing heart **when I come to you in humility as a little child so that I may understand your ways.**
Declare truth, and receive your treasure.
God, I ask you with sincerity and humility to give me a "**hearing heart**" to understand your ways.

How has your new sight changed your understanding of God?
What do you hear God saying to you?

Journal

Still the Noise

There arose a great wind storm, and the waves beat into the boat, so much that the boat was already filled. He himself was in the stern, asleep on the cushion, and they woke him up, and told him, "Teacher, don't you care that we are dying?" He awoke, and rebuked the wind, and said to the sea, "Peace! Be still!" The wind ceased, and there was a great calm.

—Mark 4:37 (WEB)

We live in a world filled with demands and stress. One Sunday, our pastor said to the community, "**Change your structure.**" Once again, I did not know what that meant, so I began the process of inquiring of God. In my younger years, I had developed a pattern of procrastination. It was the result of someone's expectation of me to perform to their standard, but when I didn't know how to do what they were asking of me, I placed it aside and waited for something to happen.

Since I have been journeying with God, I have learned to handle this situation much differently. Just prior to writing this book, I had been spending some time in Colossians. It became my "go to" book.

> *Christ is all, and in all.* **Put on** *therefore, as God's chosen ones, holy and beloved, a heart of compassion, kindness, lowliness, humility, and perseverance.* (Colossians 3:12 WEB)

My first thought was *Well, that sounds overwhelming.* Then God said, "Put on a heart of compassion." *Okay, that sounds better! Thank you, Lord. Show me how to put on a heart of compassion.* Now every time my pastor gives us instruction, I run to God and ask him to show me how to do that thing one step at a time.

God responds in his timing and in his way, which is always the perfect time and perfect way.

The following is the report I sent to the pastor a week later:

> A week ago, I was communicating with someone throughout her difficult day. At the end of the day the issue had been resolved but she indicated that her peace came as a result of receiving something that "she needed."
>
> As I read her text it hit my spirit that something was not properly aligned in her thinking. Maybe she did not mean it as I heard it but it started a process of inquiry in me.
>
> It reminded me that I often use the phrase "I need to" go to the grocery store, I need to fix dinner, I need to lose weight and the list goes on and on and on. So, I began asking myself why I use the phrase "I need" so often.
>
> I began to think about the structure of my life. My structure has always been laid out for me by someone else. First it was my parents, then my first husband and then Jerry. I learned that it was my duty to define my structure within that structure created by someone else and to act accordingly.
>
> Therefore, all "my needs" **came from my perception** of my tasks. For decades God has been a part of my life which then fit into my already defined structure.

I read about Christ in Colossians—that **by Him all things were created**…all things have been created by Him and for Him. And He is before all things and **in Him all things hold together.** That means He holds me together. So, if I am in Him then **Christ is my structure**!!! In Him I can find all the hidden treasures of wisdom and knowledge.

> **He holds my life together because my life is in Him and He is the life in me.**

Now I will return to where I started. My pastor has an apostolic grace to open blind eyes to give us the ability to see differently. The process of inquiry led to more knowledge and understanding. Then God highlighted his present-day demand on my life to put on a heart of compassion which led me to make a declaration: "I put on a heart of compassion."

How do I do that, Lord? He said, "Write a book. I will show you how to do that one step at a time. **I will make a way where there is no way.**" And he is always faithful to do what he says he will do.

Jesus calms the storm with, "Hush, be still!"

I have never written a book before. When I get stuck, I say, "What is impossible here is possible there," meaning it is not possible in my flesh, but it is possible in my spirit. That gives me peace and "stills the noise" of doubt and confusion.

Declaration of faith: God, you are the author of my life and will always help me through anything one step at a time. You will make a way where there is no way.

- ❖ Watson, what is your present-day structure?

Do you function from an external structure or from the internal structure of your core?

(As we journey, we will continue to define *structure* later in the book.)

Watson, what is the nature of God?
Watson, what is the kingdom principle you hear?

The challenge: "Game on"

By this time, you have made it on to the enemy's radar. Jesus describes it this way:

> ***The thief only comes to steal, kill, and destroy.*** *I came that they may have life, and may have it abundantly.* (John 10:10 WEB)

Satan is the enemy of God. He comes to plunder, to steal our knowledge, wisdom, and understanding of the abundant life which has been given to us in Christ Jesus.

So when you started making declarations of faith, the enemy said, "Game on," but this is no game. His goal is to destroy us. It is war. His weapons of choice are lies and deception. He is the "accuser of the brethren" (Revelation 12:10), but know that Christ is our mediator, our high priest going before God on our behalf, proclaiming that we are forgiven of all sin. Christ has already taken the punishment for us on the cross.

Our greatest weapons to break the power of the enemy over us are **worship and thanksgiving**. Worship is acknowledging and declaring your adoration and reverence to God—that he is your one true God. It is bowing your knee before him. It is declaring to the heavens the majesty and magnificence of who he is. This requires **knowledge**.

Thanksgiving is thanking God for his ways and his promises to us. This requires **wisdom** to know his ways and principles.

But then comes **understanding and strategy**.

> *Through your precepts, I get understanding; Therefore I hate every false way.* (Psalm 119:104 WEB)

> *With your instruction, I understand life; that's why I hate false propaganda.* (Psalm 119:104 The Message)

So, the first thing to do is look to see what kind of weapons you have available in your arsenal.

You have made eleven declarations of faith:

1. God, I set my mind on things above. I strain heavenward and die to my will in order to seek your will for my life.
2. Heavenly Father, as I gain more sight of you, I believe you will increase my faith so that I may be pleasing to you.
3. God, I will seek first your kingdom and your righteousness.
4. God, I believe if I call to you that you will answer me and show me great and mighty things I do not know. I believe I am your battle axe, and with me, you will break the nations of the world.

5. I put my trust in God, and I am not afraid of what man can do to me. God, I will pour out my heart to you and take refuge in you.
6. God, I will abide in your Word so that I shall know the truth to set me free.
7. God, by faith I will build a present-day structure for a future event.
8. God, I submit to the grace to build that flows from Jesus Christ.
9. God, I believe you sent Jesus into the world to save me and that you will do a new thing in me.
10. Father God, I acknowledge your sovereignty over all creation. I am your servant and come to you as a little child in need of a hearing heart to understand your ways.
11. God, you are the author of my life and will always help me through anything one step at a time. You will make a way where there is no way.

You have asked for ten treasures of knowledge and wisdom:

- A mind set on things above
- Increased faith to be pleasing to God
- A pure heart to see God
- Knowledge of true identity
- Trust in God
- Set free to abide in truth, receive wisdom, and get understanding

  - Discernment to know God's plan and purpose
  - An abundance of grace
  - Wisdom to build accurately
  - A hearing heart to understand God's ways

WHEN YOU ARE UNDER ATTACK, RUN INTO GOD.

Let's look at what David did in Psalm 77 when he was feeling overwhelmed:

> My voice rises to God, and I will cry aloud… In the day of my trouble **I sought the Lord.** (vv. 1–2)

He runs to God.

> **I will meditate with my heart.** (vv. 2–6)

He speaks from his soul confessing that he can find no comfort there.

> **And my spirit ponders.** (vv. 6–9)

Then he shifts to search the spirit and questions God, asking God if he has rejected him and withdrawn his favor from him. David is grieved because he does not feel the compassion and closeness of God.

> And finally to "still the noise" he makes a choice to meditate on the goodness and power of God. (v. 11)

> **I will meditate on all Your work** and muse on Your deeds. (v. 12)

Then he begins to worship God.

> Your way O God, is holy; **What god is great like our God? You are the God who works wonders;** You have made known Your

strength among the peoples. You have by Your power redeemed Your people. (vv. 13–15)

David has shifted his sight from his own weakness and inadequacy to the sight of God's greatness and redemptive power in order to "still the noise."

God is watching you and watching over you. He will not allow the enemy to overtake you. He will provide a way out.

With this first skirmish, God is teaching you how to use your weapons of warfare.

> *Above all,* ***taking up*** <u>***the shield of faith***</u>***, with which you will be able to quench all the fiery darts of the evil one.*** (Ephesians 6:16 WEB)

Remember all your declarations of faith. That is your shield. Take your thoughts captive, and shield them from the enemy to **"still the noise."**

> The source of noise is **fear**

The challenge

At the close of each section, you will be faced with a challenge which requires you to pull together what you have learned so far.

Your challenge is to **write a psalm** using the pattern set forth in Psalm 77:1–15. Use the notes above to guide you.

1. Lift your voice to God.
2. Pour out your heart to him; tell him what is troubling you.

3. Wrestle with God. You feel one thing but recognize it conflicts with what you know to be true.
4. Worship God and tell of his character and deeds. (Go back into the previous lessons, and pull from what you have learned about the nature of God. <u>This is not just a list. This is what you know to be true in your heart.</u>

Ask God to give you a revelation of knowledge and wisdom for your present situation then record it.

Journal: Write psalm here.

Well done, Watson!

Now you may collect your reward and move on to the next mountain.

Your reward is the **shield of faith**.

> *Now faith is the assurance of things hoped for, the conviction of things not seen.* (Hebrews 11:1 NAS)

The shield of faith stands tall the length of your body. It shields your head and your heart. Faith is knowing something to be true and committing yourself to it.

The outward side of the shield is your commitment to move forward in the ways of the Lord. The inside part of the shield is holding on to what you believe, what you know to be true about God.

Come along, Watson! When I told you to set your mind on things above, I did not mean to stick your head in the clouds. The kingdom of heaven is real with real spiritual laws.

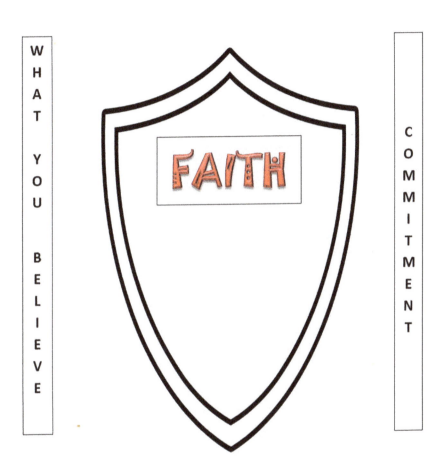

Watson, take hold of your sword and the shield and bring along the treasure chest.
It's time to journey to the next mountain.

IV

Begin Anew

https://www.youtube.com/watch?v=klbM_tAAXwg
(Go to YouTube to watch the short video.)

Monarch Butterfly Emerging from a Chrysalis

Searching for Identity

In the last section, we jackhammered up your former foundation and laid a new one. Now we will begin to build on that foundation.

My husband and I bought our first house when I was twenty-two years old. Shortly after moving in, I asked my mother to help me put in a flower garden across the front of the house on each side of the front porch. I have continued planting gardens around every home I have owned with each garden increasing in size.

I was telling someone about my love of flowers and gardening.

He asked, "Are you a master gardener?"

I replied, "No, I am just a persistent seed planter and a persevering weed puller. God is the Master Gardner. God provides the light, the rain, and power to grow and become what God has genetically coded the flower to be."

*****

At the time of the diagnosis of the disease in my body, I had been actively pursuing God for two years. I had been attending church and weekly Bible studies, traveled to Israel, had a close group of supportive women who prayed for each other, lived in a beautiful home with a panoramic view of the ocean, and outwardly led a life that looked blessed beyond measure.

But inwardly I was a mess. I was striving to find my identity, trying to understand how my childhood years had shaped me and discover the woman who God had made me to be.

I was diligent in my search, but circumstances were tossing me to and fro. The condition of my daughter's infantile hypoglycemia was improving, and I loved being a mother, but I was struggling in my marriage. Then the foundation of my beautiful home began gradually sliding down the slope of the hill, resulting in our filing a lawsuit against the builder. For the next five years, we documented the movement of the house, and we were just about to receive our court date.

I was still battling bouts of internal bleeding and taking steroid medication to control the bleeding when we received the good news that the builder had agreed to buy our house back at market value.

The same weekend we had signed a contract to buy a new home, we learned that my husband's company had had a hostile stock takeover, would not honor the pilot's contract, and would be moving the hub to another state.

The pilots went on strike, and I stayed behind in a rental house for the next six months while the girls finished their school year. Then I joined my husband in Texas, the state of my birth and the state where my extended family was located.

I didn't know it then, but God was preparing me for some life-changing events. My husband had tried a couple of new jobs but was very unhappy, which added to the stress I was already feeling. One day he returned home from work to say he was divorcing me and would be listing the house for sale the following day. Then he proceeded to move all his clothes to the guest bedroom closet. I was so shocked I just shut down and didn't even say anything. It took almost two years to finalize the divorce. We were married twenty-four years. After the divorce, I was more determined than ever to become whole, to pursue God and my true identity.

> *Therefore if anyone is in Christ, he is a new creation. The old things have passed away. Behold, all things have become new.* (2 Corinthians 5:17 WEB)

I remarried and began rebuilding the structure of my life, which included getting a job as an administrative church secretary. My boss, a very kind, caring, patient pastor, provided an environment for me to "begin anew" even though his church was not the church that I attended.

Meanwhile I entered another crisis with my health. For two to three months, everything I ate seemed to go right through me. It was getting serious, and I called my sister and told her that I was really not doing well physically. She said she knew a Christian counselor that was somewhat different in her approach, and she believed she could help me. The only problem was that she no longer lived in San Antonio, where my sister lived, but had moved to Colorado. I told Martha, my sister, that I was not able to make it to Colorado. She asked, "Do you think you are able to drive to San Antonio?"

The counselor agreed to come to San Antonio for two weeks. In the evenings and weekends, she would stay with a friend. My sister was caring for my mother, who lived with her because my mom had had a stroke resulting in short-term memory loss.

I completed a long questionnaire and met with the counselor daily. It wasn't a psychoanalyst type of counseling but biblical-based counseling. The first week, she observed me within the family dynamics of my sister and mother. Martha and Mom then left on a planned trip for a week.

This gave the counselor and me one-on-one time, and she began questioning me regarding some of her observations, giving me insight and making recommendations. I was left alone for the weekend and decided to walk to the nearby blockbuster to rent a movie. I rented *Ever After*, a version of Cinderella.

When it was over, God said to me, "You are not a caterpillar. You are a butterfly." It sounds so simple, but it greatly impacted my thinking. I knew what God was saying. The vile stuff that had been pouring from my body was actually God purging me of all the lies that had been told to me all the days of my life, defining who I was and who I should be.

God knew me and formed me in my mother's womb and wrote the days of my life ordained for me in his book before I was even born. **Only our heavenly Father has the right to define our identity.**

> *I will give thanks to you, for I am fearfully and wonderfully made. Your works are wonderful. My soul knows that very well. My frame wasn't hidden from you, when I was made in secret, woven together in the depths of the earth. Your eyes saw my body. In your book they were all written, the days that were ordained for me, when as yet there were none of them.* (Psalm 139:14–16 WEB)

Declaration of faith: God, you made me. All your works are wonderful. I was in your heart and mind before I even entered my mother's womb. You have a plan for my life, and only you can define me.

❖ Do you want to know your true identity?

What is the nature of God that you see?
God sees everything and is everywhere. His works are wonderful. God made you and me. He knows the beginning and the end.

What is the kingdom principle you hear?
God says we are fearfully and wonderfully made. Nothing is hidden from God. He gave us a soul and planned our lives.

Enter Christ into search for inquiry.

> *But all things are of God*, who reconciled us to himself through *Jesus Christ*, and gave to us the ministry of reconciliation; namely, *that God was in Christ reconciling the world to himself*, not reckoning to them their trespasses,

and having committed to us the word of reconciliation. (2 Corinthians 5:18–19 WEB)

> *Reconcile* means to reunite. God has given us access to himself through Jesus Christ, who died for our sins.
>
> What does it mean to be a new creation? This refers particularly to the heart. We are united with Christ at a heart level. By faith Christ is dwelling in our heart.
>
> We no longer know about Jesus in our flesh; we have been restored to know Christ as our true identity made in the likeness of his Father. Now we can discern the truth of what that looks like.
>
> We are anointed by the Holy Spirit with power to change from the inside out. God did this. It was his plan to unite us so we are able to have an intimate relationship with him.

Worship and thanksgiving prayer

Thank you, God, that you reconciled the world to yourself through Jesus Christ. Your works are wonderful, and I am fearfully and wonderfully made in your image. My soul longs to know you more.

Declare truth to receive your treasure:
God, only you have the right to define me because you made me. I ask for the anointing of the Holy Spirit to have **power to begin anew**.

Power to Begin Anew

How has your new sight changed your understanding of God?

What do you hear God saying to you?

Journal

A Time of Restoration

The Word became flesh, and lived among us. We saw his glory, such glory as of the one and only Son of the Father, **full of grace and truth**.

—John 1:14 (WEB)

Jesus answered him, "Most assuredly, I tell you, unless one is born anew, he can't **see the Kingdom of God**.*"*

—John 3:3

In the journey to discover our true identity, one must know his/her true father. **God is spirit and eternal**. The flesh is temporal and decaying.

I was taught that I was body, soul, and spirit—all equal importance, each with a different function. My sight changed to see myself as a spirit, housed in a temporary tent with a will and personality of my own.

The life in me and in you is Spirit. Peter refers to it as being *born again, not of corruptible seed, but of incorruptible, through the word of God, which lives and remains forever* (1 Peter 1:23 WEB).

Jesus said,

> *That which is born of the flesh is flesh.* **That which is born of the Spirit is spirit.** (John 3:6)

Aha, the identity of the Spirit in me is my true identity, but what is the DNA of that spirit? What does he look like?

God said, "Let us make man in our image, after our likeness…"

God said "our image," not "my image." God is three in one, each with a different purpose but working in relation to each other. So our spirit is in the likeness of God, Christ, and the Holy Spirit. That is our first clue. **God is relational**, so in order to discover our true identity, we must nurture a relationship with God our heavenly Father, with Christ his Son through whom we have been redeemed, and with the Holy Spirit, our counselor and guide who teaches us to discern the things of the spirit.

> *But we received, not the spirit of the world, but the Spirit which is from God, that we might know the things that were freely given to us by God which things also we speak, not in words which man's wisdom teaches, but which the Holy Spirit teaches, comparing spiritual things with spiritual things.* (1 Corinthians 2:12–13)

Declaration of faith: My true identity is "I Am Spirit." God, you are my Father and my Creator.

- ❖ Have you been born again?
- ❖ Do you want to receive your heavenly prayer language from the Holy Spirit?

What is the nature of God that you see?
God is Spirit and eternal. God is relational. Christ is full of grace and truth.

What is the kingdom principle you hear?
That which is born of the Spirit is spirit.
Enter *Holy Spirit* into search for inquiry.

> *When he had said this, he breathed on them, and said to them, "Receive the **Holy Spirit**!* **(John 20:22 WEB)**

> *They were all <u>filled with the **Holy Spirit**</u>, and <u>began to speak with other languages, as the Spirit gave them the ability to speak</u>.* **(Acts 2:4 WEB)**

SEEKING HIDDEN TREASURES | 89

But you, beloved, keep building up yourselves on your most holy faith, praying in the Holy Spirit. **(Jude 20 WEB)**

But the Counselor, the Holy Spirit, whom the Father will send in my name, he will teach you all things, and will remind you of all that I said to you. **(John 14:26 WEB)**

> The **Holy Spirit** is the third person of the Trinity—Father, Son, and Holy Spirit. He exercises the power of the Father and the Son in creation and redemption.
> It is through the power of the Holy Spirit that we are born again to receive Christ as Lord and Savior and have faith to begin anew.
> He guides believers into all truth with what he hears from the Father and the Son.
>
> *When the Counselor (Comforter) has come, whom I will send to you from the Father, the Spirit of truth, who proceeds from the Father, he will testify about me.* **(John 15:26 WEB)**

Worship and thanksgiving prayer

God, I praise you that you are a relational God. Thank you that you desire a relationship with me and that you have sent your Holy Spirit to lead me into all truth.

Declare truth to receive your treasure:

> *But to us, God revealed them through the Spirit. For the Spirit searches all things, yes, the deep things of God.* **(1 Corinthians 2:10 WEB)**

God, I am never left alone. I ask you to **fill me with the Holy Spirit** that I may perceive the deep things of God and know the mystery of Christ praying your perfect will, plans, and purpose for my life.

Filled with Holy Spirit

What is a heavenly language?
When you pray in your heavenly language, it bypasses your mind and is a direct communication spirit to spirit from you to God. Therefore, you know that you are praying God's perfect will for your life. It is a gift.

> *I tell you, keep asking, and it will be given you. Keep seeking, and you will find. Keep knocking, and it will be opened to you.* **For everyone who asks receives**. *He who seeks finds. To him who knocks it will be opened. "Which of you fathers, if your son asks for bread, will give him a stone? Or if he asks for a fish, he won't give him a snake instead of a fish, will he? Or if he asks for an egg, he won't give him a scorpion, will he? If*

> *you then, being evil, know how to give good gifts to your children, how much more will your heavenly Father give the Holy Spirit to those who ask him?"* **(Luke 11:9–13 WEB)**

Jesus said you will receive power when the Holy Spirit comes upon you. To pray in another language is evidence of the baptism of the Holy Spirit.

> *They were all filled with the Holy Spirit, and began to speak with other languages, as the Spirit gave them the ability to speak.* **(Acts 2:4 WEB)**

> *For he who speaks in another language speaks not to men, but to God; for no one understands; but in the Spirit he speaks mysteries.* **(1 Corinthians 14:2 WEB)**

Prayer to ask to receive your heavenly language

Father God, when Jesus ascended into heaven, he said, "I am sending forth the promise of my Father upon you," and you say that everyone who asks (according to your will) receives, so I am asking for the promise of the baptism of the Holy Spirit and your gift of my heavenly prayer language.

Use my tongue and my voice to glorify you. I believe that I have received. Help me to speak it and practice as I pray. (Open your mouth and begin to speak. It may sound like Babel or gibberish at first, but then you will have more confidence with practice.) Pray in your heavenly language when you feel like you do not know what to pray or how to pray. It will edify you, strengthen you, and give you peace.

God Is Sovereign

***Worthy** are you, our Lord and God, the **Holy** One, to **receive the glory, the honor, and the power**, for **you created all things**, and because of your desire they existed, and were created!*
—Revelation 4:11 (WEB)

One of the women in my church had invited a speaker to come to town and speak at a weekend conference. As I listened, I knew there was something different about the way he talked. God was drawing me closer into Christ. I later discovered this man had an apostolic grace on him to open my blind eyes, tear down the old structure, and build a new one within me.

*****

To say that God created us and formed us in our mother's womb is saying that we submit to his sovereign power. He is our Creator, which **gives him the right to define how we function, think, and feel.**

> The pattern of the seven days of Creation in Genesis shows that God is **ordered and structured**. He is not random, but creates and builds day-by-day, layer upon layer. (DNW)

So we learn that **God's process has sequence and strategic action**. He builds our internal core in this same way. He is orderly, evaluates things, and is not random or arbitrary. He has a strategic plan for the life of each one of his children.

In the Bible, when the Lord tells Habakkuk about his judgment upon Judah and the impending invasion of the Babylonian army, Habakkuk's first response is "I heard, and my inward parts trembled." But later he submits to the sovereignty of God and says, "Yet I will exult in the Lord. I will rejoice in the God of my salvation. **The Lord is my strength**."

I remember the day my daughter called to say that she had been to the doctor for an ultrasound and she was pregnant with twin boys. I was elated. We waited with anticipation for their birth. The day arrived, but there was a complication with the birthing process. The first baby came out but brought the placenta with him, which meant his brother was not getting any oxygen. The doctor frantically tried to reach him but could find only one leg and one arm because he had popped up to the top of the uterus in a lateral position.

The doctor asked my daughter, "What do you want me to do?"

She replied, "Do whatever you have to do."

That meant he performed a crash caesarian section to deliver the baby within three minutes, rapidly cutting her open to save the baby's life. Because the placenta had been prematurely ripped from her body, the bleeding was not stopping. The doctor told her and her husband that if they had anything to say to each other, now was the time—meaning if the bleeding continued, she would not live through it. Praise God it finally did stop, and she survived the two-and-a-half-hour surgery to put her back together. The second boy came out blue but survived the ordeal also, and we had our twin boys.

Of course, I thought they were the cutest little identical twins ever. Time passed. They were constant companions with the one always watching over the other. They were not talking but we thought maybe that was just a twin thing. They seemed to have an understanding between them, a way of communicating, but it did appear that they experienced more than the usual number of emotional meltdowns. They had some difficulty adjusting to preschool, but that also improved some with time.

About the time the boys turned three, my daughter took them to the elementary school speech therapist for an evaluation. After a fifteen-minute assessment, the speech therapist gave my daughter a checklist and told her the boys would not be eligible for services at the local elementary school. They would have to be seen at a regional center ninety minutes away due to their new diagnosis. My daughter called me in tears to say that the woman had told her that the boys were autistic, would never speak, would never read, and would never graduate from high school.

It was shocking news and very distressing. After gathering my thoughts, I turned to God with tears coming down my cheeks and said, "Lord, I give to you that which is most precious to me. I praise your holy name. You are my sovereign God."

I heard him say in a still quiet voice inside my spirit, "**I will make a way where there is no way**."

I put my trust in God to make provision for their journey through life. Eighteen years have passed since their birth, and God has opened doors for them in miraculous ways, step by step. They are speaking. They are in school. They are able to read. The second twin had some special resource classes, and they both had tutors after school for many years. It is not easy for their family, but I have a grateful heart for God's mercy, favor, strength, provision, and wisdom in the midst of the crisis. Their journey has pioneered new ways in the school systems where they have attended and opened the eyes of their educators to see special-needs children in a new light. Their first teacher in preschool did not want them in her class but later had a change of heart. After seeing their progress, she told their mother that she had not yet completed her teacher education and she would be changing her major to teach special children. My daughter sees the boys as ambassadors touching the hearts of people and making a way for other special kids to follow where there was no way before.

The apostolic grace has a pioneering dimension to make a way for others to follow in search of God's will and plan in the earth. We are journeying to the finish.

The sovereignty of God had become my operating environment. God was establishing a proper foundation in me and showing me how to respond in the midst of crisis. He was teaching me to respond from a foundation of truth and relationship with him rather than out of fear and emotion.

> For God didn't give us a spirit of fear, but of power, love, and self-control. (2 Timothy 1:7 WEB)

Declaration of faith: Your sovereignty is my operating environment. God, you are sovereign over all things. You have the right to define how I function, think, and feel.

❖ Do you submit your life to your sovereign Creator and give him the right to define how you function, think, and feel?

What is the nature of God that you see?
God is holy. He is worthy to receive glory, honor, and power. He is the creator of all things. He is ordered and structured.

What is the kingdom principle you hear?
It is God who gives us a spirit of power, love, and self-control. Because God created us, he has the right to define how we function, think, and feel.

Enter Fear into search for inquiry.

> In the fear of the LORD is strong confidence: and his children shall have a place of refuge. (Proverbs 14:26 Webster)

> A healthy fear of God is to have reverence or respect. Awe arises out of admiration for his character. A well-disciplined child will

> have strong confidence in his father's mercy and goodness and dread that which might displease him.
> *The fear of the LORD is a fountain of life.* (Proverbs 14:27) (Webster)
>
> Fear of the Lord is spiritual life which springs from him, is supported by him, and maintained through him. God is a high tower. To fear him is a safe place to be.

Worship and thanksgiving prayer

God, you are sovereign over all your creation. It is because of your desire that all things exist. You are worthy to receive glory, honor, and power. Thank you that you are a fountain of life to us.

Declare truth to receive your treasure:
You are a holy God. I pray for a reverent **"fear of the Lord."**

How has your new sight changed your understanding of God?
What do you hear God saying to you?

Journal

God Is Our Keeper

I will lift up my eyes to the hills—from whence comes my help? My help comes from the Lord, who **made heaven and earth.** *He will not allow your foot to be moved;* **He who keeps you will not slumber**. *Behold, He who keeps Israel shall neither slumber nor sleep.* **The Lord is your keeper**; *the Lord is your shade at your right hand. The sun shall not strike you by day, nor the moon by night.* **The Lord shall preserve you from all evil; He shall preserve your soul**. *The Lord shall preserve your going out and your coming in from this time forth, and even forevermore.*
—Psalm 121:1–8 (NKJV)

Yesterday I was driving the fifteen-mile stretch of highway into town to go to work. Before I knew it, I was being signaled by the state trooper to pull over because he caught me speeding. That is never a good feeling. He came to the right front window and said that he would have to give me a citation for going eighty-four miles an hour in a seventy-mile-an-hour speed zone and asked for my driver's license.

I said, "I know you are right—I was not thinking. My mind was elsewhere."

I couldn't tell him that the reason my mind was elsewhere was because I was deep in thought about the book and asking God, "Where do you want me to journey next in the book?"

The officer was very professional; he returned to his car to put my information into the computer. While I was waiting, I began to think about him. He had authority to administer the law, was equipped with a gun and other tools to handle rebellion, and seemed well able to do so, yet there was a kindness beneath the surface. All of a sudden, I was overtaken with compassion for him and his job. I was praying and asking God as to what God would want me to say. About eight minutes later, the officer returned to the left window and apologized for taking so long. He explained that his computer had crashed and he would not keep me any longer but would send the citation by mail. By that time, I was in tears, but it was not because of the citation.

I said, "I would like to tell you something."

He braced himself on the door as he leaned in and turned his ear toward me. The road noise was loud, and I also was having difficulty speaking.

Finally, I put my hand on his forearm and said, "I am so thankful for you and for the job that you do along with your fellow officers. You put your life on the line every day to keep us safe. Tell them how much I appreciate it and that there are more of us than there are of them."

He knew to whom I was referring—the cop haters who have been protesting and the murders of policemen this past year.

He thanked me and said, "It is people like you that keep us going."

I was kind of weepy the rest of the day. Finally, I said, "Wow, God, what was that all about? What are you showing me?"

I was guilty of breaking the law, but instead of feeling guilt, shame, and rejection, my heart was overcome with grace to have compassion for another.

Grace is unconditional love and acceptance. It is the unmerited favor of God toward his children.

> **For God so loved the world**, that he gave his only-begotten Son, that whosoever believes on him may not perish, but have life eternal.

The grace of God was revealed and given in the person and work of Jesus Christ, who is the embodiment of grace bringing salvation to mankind. By his death and resurrection, Jesus restored the broken fellowship between God and his people.

We all fall short of the glory of God. When I was speeding, I had broken the law, but the covenant of grace intervened to restore my relationship with God and with others.

Declaration of faith: I believe that you gave your Son to me so I might have eternal life. You preserve me from evil, and you preserve my soul. You are the keeper of my soul, and you keep me safe.

- ❖ Do you live under the law trying to prove you are worthy of God's love through performance?
- ❖ Or do you receive God's unconditional love and forgiveness through the covenant of grace?

What is the nature of God that you see?
God made heaven and earth. He does not slumber. He is the keeper of our soul and keeps us from evil.
What is the kingdom principle you hear?
Because God loved the world, he made a way to give us eternal life through Jesus. Jesus Christ is the fullness of God's grace to us.

Enter *grace* into search for inquiry.

> He has said to me, "My *grace* is sufficient for you, for my power is made perfect in weakness." Most gladly therefore I will rather glory in my weaknesses, that **the power of Christ may rest on me**. **(2 Corinthians 12:9 WEB)**

> This is a very practical promise from God. When you are faced with a situation that is overwhelming to you, look up for help. God will make a way where there is no way when we humble ourselves before God to say, "Lord, I cannot do this, but you can. I am weak, but you are strong. God, I believe that your grace is sufficient for me and your power is made perfect in my weakness."

Worship and thanksgiving prayer

God, you made heaven and earth. You do not slumber. Thank you that you are the keeper of my soul. You keep me safe from evil.

Declare truth to receive your treasure:
God, I ask you for **sufficient grace** that the power of Christ may rest on me as the Holy Spirit comes to aid in the preservation of my soul.

SUFFICIENT GRACE

How has your new sight changed your understanding of God?
What do you hear God saying to you?

Journal
_____

The Bond

> **Above all these things,** *walk in love,*
> *which is the bond of perfection.*
> —Colossians 3:14 (WEB)

Bond is defined as promise, pledge, oath word, connection, and union. A bond of love unites all the graces of God together and makes the system complete. (I will give you a list of graces later.)

It is absolutely necessary for relationships. Everything that God created is in relation to something else, but God says it is love that holds it all together into completion.

Colossians 2:15 says that *Jesus Christ is the image of the invisible God*, the *firstborn of all creation*.

> *For by him were all things created, in the heavens and on the earth, things visible and things invisible,* whether thrones or dominions or principalities or powers; all things have been created through him, and for him. He is before all things, and in him all things are held together. (Colossians 1:16–17 WEB)

Christ is the embodiment of all that God is, and GOD IS LOVE. In Jesus Christ we are able to see the structure of God's love. What exactly is love? Look at Jesus Christ. In Jesus and through Jesus, God gave us a promise, a pledge, an oath, and his Word that we would become one, united in love.

*****

At age five or six—I don't exactly remember which one—I went with my mother and siblings to visit my mother's cousin. After the visit, we all exited to go somewhere. Upon leaving her house, Dorothy, mom's cousin, asked if I would like to ride with her in her car. I liked her very much and felt excited about it. I asked Mom if that would be all right, and she said yes. I walked out in front of mother's car to cross the street to the other side where Dorothy's car was parked and immediately was hit by a passing car. My sister said I went flying through the air from the impact and landed on my head. My brother said it looked like I had half of a tennis ball stuck in my forehead, and my mom later told me that the wheel of the car stopped just inches from running over my head. She said the only thing that saved me was that the driver was an elderly man and was not going too fast.

I was knocked unconscious, but I still remember part of it. I remember crying on the inside while I lay on my mother's lap as Dorothy drove to the emergency room at the hospital. I remember being in a lot of pain as they cut the clothes off my body and placed me face down on the egg protruding from my forehead so they could take an x-ray. I remember feeling extreme cold until mother asked them to put a blanket on me. I remember nothing more about the incident except being at home, wearing a cast from my neck to my waist, and being afraid to walk in the street.

Despite of the trauma, which stayed with me for many years, God worked it for good. Deep within me, the incident created a bond with God. Thankfully, I had suffered only a broken collarbone and a concussion. It should have been so much worse. I believed God saved me for his good pleasure and purpose. I saw it as a pledge that he would love me and keep me as the apple of his eye until completion.

The apostle Paul said,

> *For I am confident of this very thing, that **He who began a good work in you will perfect it until the day of Christ Jesus***. (Philippians 1:6)

> *Work out your own salvation with fear and trembling; for **it is God who works in you both to will and to do for His good pleasure**.* (Philippians 2:12–13)

> We love, because he first loved us. (1 John 4:19)

Declaration of faith: God, I love you because you first loved me. I believe you will perfect the work you have begun in me. I believe Jesus Christ is the firstborn of your creation and is made in your image.

❖ Do you have a bond with God? With others?

What is the nature of God that you see?
God is perfect love. Jesus Christ is the image of the invisible God, the firstborn of all creation.

All things have been created through Jesus Christ and for him. He is before all things, and in him all things are held together.

What is the kingdom principle you hear?
God will continue to perfect the work which he has begun in us to do his will and his good pleasure.

Enter *love* into search for inquiry.

> *Jesus answered him, "**If a man loves me, he will keep my word**. My Father will **love** him, and we will come to him, and make our home with him."* (John 14:23 WEB)

> God is looking for vessels into which he can pour himself. One who keeps the Word of God is called a vessel of honor.
>
> *A vessel for honor, sanctified and useful for the Master, prepared for every good work.* (2 Timothy 2:21 NKJV)
>
> Why would a person deny himself the desires of the flesh to serve God? There is only one reason—because we love him more than we love ourselves.

Worship and thanksgiving prayer

God, you are the perfection of love. Thank you, God, that you loved us so much that you created your firstborn son in your image to demonstrate your love to us. Thank you that you will perfect the work that you have begun in us.

Declare truth to receive your treasure:

God, I ask to **walk in love**, the bond of perfection.

How has your new sight changed your understanding of God?
What do you hear God saying to you?

Journal

Arise and Shine

Arise, shine; for your light has come!
And the glory of the Lord is risen upon you.
For behold, the darkness shall cover the earth,
And deep darkness the people; but the Lord will arise over you,
And His glory will be seen upon you.
(Isaiah 60:1–2 NKJV)
(Song "Arise Shine for Your Light Has Come")

During the two years that I was in limbo, waiting to see if the divorce would really happen, I began to reevaluate my life. Where had I taken the wrong path? I went to a local Christian counselor to gain sight and understanding. After a couple of sessions, I was awakened from slumber to see that my boundaries were so broken down.

The book of Nehemiah is a book about covenant, compassion, and restoration. God had passed judgment on the people of Judah because of their disobedience. Many were killed, but others were taken captive and carried back into the Babylonian empire for seventy years. Prior to the book of Nehemiah, some Jews had returned to Judah, being led by Ezra. Thirteen years later, another group returned, led by Zerubbabel. Ninety-four years later, Nehemiah, who held the position of cup bearer to the king of Persia, hears a report that the walls of Jerusalem are broken down and the gates burned with fire.

Without walls, Jerusalem (the spiritual and political center of Judah) could hardly be considered a city at all. Nehemiah prays to God and reminds God of his covenant with his chosen people, that they were to be the place where his name would dwell. Nehemiah pleads with God to have compassion on them.

Once again, **God makes a way where there is no way.** God gives Nehemiah favor with the king, who then gives him permission to return to Judah along with provision and protection for the massive project of rebuilding the walls.

Nehemiah inspects the walls and challenges the people to "arise and build." The building begins immediately, and despite of great opposition from both inside and outside, the wall is completed in just fifty-two days.

Nehemiah records that when the enemies heard of it and all the surrounding nations saw it, they lost their confidence, for they recognized that the work had been accomplished with the help of his God.

*****

I had asked my first husband to go with me to my next appointment with the counselor. While we were there, I asked him if he was willing to do anything to make our marriage better.

He said, "No."

I said, "Well, that is what I thought, but I wanted to hear you say it before a witness."

I knew then that we were traveling on divergent paths. I rose up to make a declaration: "I am going to get whole and healthy no matter what it takes."

First, with God's help, I was taking responsibility to rebuild my personal boundaries. Because of God saving my life when I was hit by the car, I bonded with God. However, it produced an opposite result with my mother. It caused a fracture in my relationship with her.

As I was healing after the incident both physically and emotionally, I do not remember receiving any comfort from my mother. She never told me that she was sorry for my pain or sorry that this had happened to me. I became confused. Did that mean I was supposed to feel guilty? Should I have known better? Was I on my own to sort through my feelings? That was the beginning of my walls breaking down. Her needs and emotions began to invade my feelings, my thoughts, and my actions which became entangled with her own brokenness.

It became the pattern for my life which had carried on into my marriage. Now I could recognize it but had no knowledge of how to shift from the imprinted pattern within me to the pattern of Jesus Christ.

> *Again, therefore, Jesus spoke to them, saying, "**I am the light of the world**. He who follows me will not walk in the darkness, but will have the* *light of life**."* (John 8:12 WEB)

Declaration of faith: God, I will arise from my slumber and choose to walk in the light of life through Jesus Christ.

- ❖ Do you want to become whole?
- ❖ Do you want to give God permission to tear down the old structure and rebuild a new structure in you—one that contains the pattern of his Son?

What is the nature of God that you see?
God is the light of life.
What is the kingdom principle you hear?
To walk in the ways of Jesus is walking in the light of life and not in darkness.
Enter *arise or awake* into search for inquiry.

> *But all things that are exposed are made manifest by the light, for whatever makes manifest is light. Therefore He says: "**Awake**, you who sleep,* *arise* *from the dead, and Christ will give you light."* (Ephesians 5:13–14 NKJV)

> Darkness is the absence of light or illumination.
>
> "Darkness cannot drive out darkness; only light can do that. Hate cannot drive out

> hate; only love can do that." Martin Luther King Jr.
>
> *Your word is a lamp to my feet, and a light for my path.* (Psalm 119:105 WEB)
>
> To walk toward the light, to walk into the light, to abide in the light is a choice.

Worship and thanksgiving prayer

God, you are light, and there is no darkness in you. Thank you for sending your son to earth to show us the light and to free us from darkness.

Declare truth to receive your treasure:
Heavenly Father, I ask for your Word to dwell in my heart and be a **light for my path**.

A Light for My Path

How has your new sight changed your understanding of God?
What do you hear God saying to you?

Journal

Sonship

Have this mind in you, which was also in Christ Jesus.
—Philippians 2:5 (ASV)

The Word says that Jesus humbled himself and became obedient to the point of death, even up until his death on the cross.

> *Jesus therefore answered them, "Most assuredly, I tell you, **the Son can do nothing of himself**, but what he sees the Father doing. For whatever things he does, these the Son also does likewise. (John 5:19 WEB)*

Jesus can do nothing of himself because he is in perfect union with his Father. The cross represents dying to our own preferences and desires in order to live, fully seeking the will of our Father to honor his name.

As we walk in union with our heavenly Father, it gives us the right to expect full favor, full partnership, full understanding, and full flow of the anointing, full maturity and development of the saints, full competence, and a full sense of the presence of God.

However, this requires our ruthless obedience, our exact obedience. When we hear the voice of God with the intent to obey, this is the process of dying to everything that is opposition to the will of God. It is the offering of oneself to God as an act of worship.

The apostle Paul said,

> *Therefore I urge you, brothers, **by the mercies of God**, to present your bodies a living sacrifice, holy, acceptable to God, which is your spiritual service. Don't be conformed to this world, but **be transformed by the renewing of your***

mind, so that you may prove what is the good, well-pleasing, and perfect will of God. (Romans 12:1–2 WEB)

Paul did not mean just our physical body for service but our body, mind, and spirit. Our goal is for confluence within us, the coming together of the parts to make the whole. It is also a convergent path to unite the triune God and the body of Christ into oneness.

Back in the seventies, I attended a church during the charismatic movement of God. We were learning about the Holy Spirit and the gifts of the Spirit. I attended a Bible study group of about one hundred women led by a charismatic teacher. She read Romans 12:1—"to present our bodies a living sacrifice"—and then asked that everyone who wanted to offer their body as a living sacrifice to stand up. I stood, and she prayed to God, acknowledging our commitment to him to offer our bodies as a living sacrifice, holy and acceptable to him in spiritual service.

At the time, I didn't fully understand what it meant to offer my body as a living sacrifice, but I knew it was well pleasing to God, so I did it as an act of worship in obedience to his Word and will. I did it as a declaration of my perfected intent in alignment with his will for my life.

Later, when I learned about the power and authority of making declarations according to the Word, I read the Bible differently.

For instance, I started making declarations as I read through Psalms. If it says, "Give thanks to the Lord for **he is good**," I read it to say, "I give you thanks, Lord, for you are good." Or when I read "Thou didst make me bold with strength in my soul," I say, "Thank you, God, that you make me bold in my soul."

I was now making declarations of truth, in faith, fully expecting to see it manifested in my life. When Paul talks about the thorn in his flesh, he says that God said to him, "My **grace** is sufficient for you, for **power** is **perfected in weakness**." Then I say,

"Thank you, God, that your grace is sufficient for me and that you are perfecting your power in my weakness."

> *Rejoice always, pray without ceasing, in everything give thanks*; for this is the will of God in Christ Jesus for you. Do not quench the Spirit. (1 Thessalonians 5:16–19 NKJV)

Paul says to *walk in Christ rooted and built up in him and* **established in the faith** *even as you were taught, abounding in it in thanksgiving.* We are established in faith by being rooted in the soil of God's love, supported through an attitude of thanksgiving and a grateful heart.

Thanksgiving gave me strength to persevere through my journey of living with an autoimmune disease. I am not thankful for the disease. I am thankful that in the midst of it, God is establishing my faith and building me in the image of his Son.

Romans 5:3–5: *But we also* ***rejoice in our sufferings***

- ***knowing that suffering works perseverance***
- ***and perseverance proven character***
- ***and proven character hope***
- ***and hope doesn't disappoint us***

BECAUSE *God's love has been poured out into our hearts through the Holy Spirit who was given to us.*

Declaration of faith: God, I pray to rejoice always, pray without ceasing, and in everything give thanks. I ask to be transformed by the renewing of my mind.

❖ Do you have a grateful heart toward God for building you in the image of his Son?

What is the nature of God that you see?
He is a God of goodness, mercy, grace, and power. He is the establisher of our faith.
What is the kingdom principle you hear?
Rejoice always, pray without ceasing, and in everything give thanks. Rejoice in our sufferings knowing it leads to perseverance, character, and hope. We can do nothing of ourselves for your power is made perfect in our weakness.
Enter *rejoice* into search for inquiry.

> *I will be glad and rejoice in your loving kindness, for you have seen my affliction. You have known my soul in adversities.* (Psalm 31:7 WEB)

> Rejoice in God's loving-kindness. He sees our pain and the troubles of our soul.
>
> And my soul shall be joyful in the LORD: it shall rejoice in his salvation. God delivers us from our enemy, from our distress, from hurtful thoughts and doubt. (Psalm 35:9 KJV)

Worship and thanksgiving prayer

Heavenly Father, you are a God of mercy and grace. Thank you that you deliver me from my enemy and restore my soul. I rejoice in your goodness and loving-kindness to me.

Declare truth to receive your treasure:
In everything I will give thanks; I ask you for **a grateful heart**.

A Grateful Heart

The challenge

Watson, write a letter of thanksgiving to God. Think about the course of your lifetime. Think about the difficult things—the hurt and pain you have gone through. Name them, lay them down at the feet of Jesus as an offering of worship. Allow Jesus to heal your emotions. Thank him for healing.

Thank God for bringing you to a place where you can begin anew. Thank him for building a new structure in you to have the mind of Christ, etc.

Thank him that you no longer feel bound by the circumstances in the earth—past and present—but feel empowered from above, and that you are no longer looking to what you want changed but feeling empowered to make changes.

Be specific.

Journal: write letter here

Well done, Watson!

Now you may collect your reward and move on to the next mountain.

Your reward is

The Helmet of Salvation

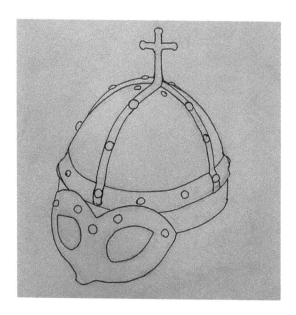

The helmet will preserve you in the day of spiritual conflict. It defends the head, a vital part containing your mind. The hope of salvation will defend your soul and keep it from the blows of the enemy.

Come along, Watson. Bring your sword, your shield, and put on your helmet. Don't forget the treasure chest. I see some dark clouds. There may be a storm brewing ahead.

V

Becoming

*When I was a child, I spoke as a child, I felt as a child, I thought as a child. Now that I have become a man, I have **put away childish things.***
—1 Corinthians 13:11 (WEB)

Maturity is being complete in growth or development. It is the ability to be fully submitted to the authority of God in Christ to come into the likeness of Christ and to take responsibility to make accurate choices to be established in the Word.

*God's definition of **maturity is the fullness of His anointing carried fully in the earth by a spiritually mature people**.* (DNW)

Maturity is a people who are so strong they cannot be moved by external influences that seek to change their directions.

Growing up is not achieved by depending on ourselves; it is not achieved by finding capacity inside of ourselves nor is it not achieved by how much we train ourselves to do well. Rather, **growing up is achieved by**

reaching up and pulling down God: God's ideas, God's capacity, God's enthusiasm, God's passion, and God's energy. (DNW)

For in just a very little while, "He who is coming will come and will not delay. ***But my righteous one will live by faith****. And if he shrinks back, I will not be pleased with him."*

We are not of those who shrink back and are destroyed but of those who believe and are saved.

Recently, I mentioned to someone close to me that **I was writing a book using my journey through illness to illustrate how to reach up to God and pull down resources from God to navigate through crisis**. He replied that he did not believe God worked like that and I had brought the sickness on myself. I began thinking about his response and thought he is right. I have made some bad choices in the past.

Then I asked him, "What about people like the Japanese who were exposed to radiation because of a tsunami or people who have recently lost their homes due to floods or fires? You are missing the point."

I continued, "I have been through a lot in the last five years. Have I ever been depressed one day? No. Have I ever thought of myself as a victim? No. There are millions of people taking drugs because they cannot cope with life. There are millions of people taking pain-killing drugs and drinking alcohol for a little relief. We live in a fallen world."

Maturity is a faith based process.

Compassion and Mercy of God

Like a father has compassion on his children, So Yahweh has compassion on those who fear him. (Psalm 103:13 WEB)

*Behold, we call them blessed who endured. You have heard of the patience of Job, and have seen the Lord in the outcome, and how **the Lord is full of compassion and mercy**.* (James 5:11)

Five years ago, I was diagnosed with breast cancer. In the three months between the diagnosis and surgery, God was giving me resource to navigate through crisis. It looked like this:

My day began with a voice message on my cell phone to call the doctor as soon as I could. I knew that meant it wasn't good news. If it is good news, they tell you on the phone. Bad news they tell you in the office. In prior weeks, I had gone in for a mammogram; I returned for a breast sonogram and then returned for a stereotactic biopsy.

My Declaration

As I entered my family practice doctor's office and the nurse told me to take a seat, I was thinking that it must be difficult for him to give bad news to people—and that is just how Dr. Sterling began: "I have some bad news and some good news. You have breast cancer, invasive ductal carcinoma…" I'm not sure what the good news was, but I sat and listened. Then I responded, "Well, I had already realized that was what you were going to tell me. I have a strong faith and a great support system." He asked where I went to church, which gave me the opportunity to explain that I was part of a worldwide Apostolic Reformation church and God had been preparing a gathering of believers for this time as we moved closer to the finish, the completion of God's purpose for mankind. **God will use this process to strengthen my core** so that we (my church community) can build God's purpose in the earth and strengthen the body of Christ. He agreed because he could see that times were getting tougher and the world was getting darker.

This was the beginning of God teaching me to live a life driven by the spirit from the inside out. It was the compassion and mercy of God to give me sight of his purpose.

After I had completed my year-long journey and had written down this process in a journal, I was able to share my process with another woman my age who was diagnosed with breast cancer. She was in that first stage of trying to make decisions.

I advised, "Carolyn, this is not about the cancer. It is about God doing a work in you and strengthening your core." She was part of our church community located in another state, and Carolyn later told me that she went to church the next Sunday and told everyone, "This is not about the cancer." Our conversation completely changed her thinking about the diagnosis and how to journey through it.

So the first set of questions to ask God when you find yourself facing a very difficult situation is as follows:

- "God, what do you want?"
- "What do you want me to learn through this?"
- "What is your purpose to be accomplished during this time?"

When you know the answer to these questions, then you will know how to posture yourself for the journey.

Declaration of faith: God, I put away childish things. I reach up and pull down your ideas, capacity, enthusiasm, passion, and energy. I will live by faith and not shrink back.

❖ Do you want God to strengthen your core?

What is the nature of God that you see?
God is a father full of compassion and mercy.
What is the kingdom principle you hear?
Remember, maturity is the fullness of his anointing carried fully in the earth by a spiritually mature people. Put away childish things. Pull down resource from God. Maturity is a faith-based process.

Enter *Compassion* into search for inquiry.

> *Jesus came out, saw a great multitude, and he had* compassion *on them,* **because they were like sheep without a shepherd**, *and he began to teach them many things.* (Mark 6:34 WEB)

SEEKING HIDDEN TREASURES

Jesus called the people "sheep." Let's look at some of the characteristics of sheep.

- They are **meek** and usually very quiet and gentle.
- They have an **obedient** character and tend to listen to the lead sheep.
- They have a gregarious social instinct that allows them to **bond closely to other sheep**.
- They **stay together as a flock** to protect themselves from predators and comfort each other.
- Sheep <u>**know the voice of their shepherd and will follow him**</u>.
- They are **quick learners** and **have good memories**.

However, sheep are not very intelligent. To call someone a sheep is to say that he/she mindlessly follows the crowd/majority without using his own brain or rationale.

They do not like change and are afraid of the unknown, of darkness and strange pastures.

Sheep have no fighting skills to defend themselves. They do not get angry, and they do not try to escape. They cannot fight back

> and are the only animals that make no noise when they die.
>
> John the Baptist said, *"Behold! The Lamb of God who takes away the sin of the world!"* (John 1:29–30 NKJV)
>
> Without the word of God to teach us, we are like sheep without a shepherd following every wind of doctrine. (Ephesians 4:14–15)
>
> *That we should no longer be children, tossed to and fro and carried about with every wind of doctrine, by the trickery of men, in the cunning craftiness of deceitful plotting, but, speaking the truth in love, may grow up in all things into Him who is the head—Christ. (NKJV)*

Worship and thanksgiving prayer

God, you are full of compassion and mercy. You have compassion on those who fear you. Thank you for the Lamb who was slain for my sin to give me a life filled with your love and bounty. Thank you for the Good Shepherd who leads us in the ways of right living and prosperity.

Declare truth to receive your treasure:
Lord, as I hear and follow your voice, I ask for your

Compassion to Learn Your Ways

How has your new sight changed your understanding of God?
What do you hear God saying to you?

Journal

Moving by the Voice of God

*And all things, whatsoever you shall ask in
prayer, believing, you shall receive.*
—Matthew 21:22

I heard in my Spirit the Father reaching out to me to communicate hope and to **ask me to trust him in all things** (Romans 8:28) *and that he would work all things together for good*.

So, I knew God's purpose was to strengthen my core, but I wasn't sure how to do that.

On the previous day, my pastor was saying to **move from believing that Christ is in me to knowing that Christ is in me.** Our core is our heart—our thinking system: our faith, obedience, commitment, sacrifice are all from our core.

Faith for the Journey

After hearing his message, I made declarations: "God, **I am core** to your plan." Dr. Woodroffe had given us six primary principles to enhance our ability to walk with God. So, I prayed these principles in the form of declarations as seen below.

Declaration of faith:

God, I **partner with your Word**, your intentions, your actions and will.

I thank you, God, that **you have given me access to your mind**.

God, I have confidence, faith, and power because **I am aligned with your intentions and desires**.

I am in perfect harmony with you, and there is no turbulence between the movement of my will and your will.

Thank you, God, that you will share information with me about your future plan because I am a son in your household. **I am informed about the things of God (Sonship)**.

Thank you, God, that you have revealed yourself to me, and **I understand and have knowledge of your nature and your ways**.

❖ Do you trust God in all things?

What is the nature of God that you see?
God is all powerful. He knows the way. He provides the light in the darkness.

What is the kingdom principle you hear?
Ask anything in alignment with God's will, plan, and purpose. Believe that you have received.

Enter *Know* into search for inquiry.

> *Be still and **know** that I am God. I will be exalted among the nations. I will be exalted in the earth.* (Psalm 46:10 WEB)

> Our part is to "**be still**." That means do not be anxious but instead leave the matter with God. Let God do what only God can accomplish. If I focused on the cancer, I would be missing the point. Instead, I asked God what was it that he wanted to accomplish in me as I journeyed through the process of cancer.
>
> God said that he would be exalted in the earth (in you and in me). He is saying his power is made perfect in our weakness. Give God a chance to show off and then praise him for his might and counsel.

Worship and thanksgiving prayer

God, I exalt you in all the earth. Nothing is impossible for you. Thank for revealing yourself to me and giving me counsel in the midst of crisis.
Declare truth to receive your treasure:

God, I ask you for **strength in my core**.

How has your new sight changed your understanding of God?
What do you hear God saying to you?

Journal

Positioned My Heart

Being confident of this very thing, that he who began a good work in you will complete it until the day of Jesus Christ.
—Philippians 1:6 (WEB)

So, I **positioned my heart** to see the process of living through breast cancer as a spiritual journey. I looked for patterns of courage and understanding of God's ways in the Bible.

I was reminded that God is redemptive and that he can use **what the enemy means for evil and turn it around for good**. I thought about Joseph and how the enemy took him from his father into a foreign land. Yet it was God's plan all along to save Jacob's family and build them into a nation.

> *And God sent me before you to preserve you a remnant in the earth and to save you alive by a great deliverance.* (Genesis 45:7)

I thought about the religious Jews who believed that they had destroyed Jesus on the cross. Three days later, he was resurrected and completed the purpose for which God had sent him into the earth. Because I had experienced God leading me for many years, I knew God was not done with me yet.

Appropriated Strength

I felt reassured again that God had a plan and purpose for my life. The Lord says, "**Be strong and of good courage**." This is what Moses said to the Israelites.

> *Then Moses called Joshua and said to him in the sight of all Israel, "**Be strong and of good courage**, for you must go with this people to the land which the Lord has sworn to their fathers to give them and you shall cause them to inherit it.* ***And the Lord,*** **He is the One who goes before you. He will be with you**; *He will not leave you nor forsake you; do not fear nor be dismayed."* (Deuteronomy 31:7 NKJV)

Armed with new strength, I researched on the Internet the type of cancer that I had and prepared to meet the surgeon to find out more. My husband accompanied me to see the surgeon. The diagnosis was stage one cancer, but it would be upgraded if my lymph nodes had cancer.

As he continued, I became confused and kept asking my husband, "What did he say?"

He had been a general surgeon in the military, and I found his attitude to be cavalier and lacking in compassion. He said, "It would be a one-and-half-hour surgery, and I could go back to work the next day."

I left the office dismayed. I knew he was not the right surgeon for me.

Declaration of faith: God, you are a God who finishes what you start. You have a strategic plan to strengthen my core, and I know you will be with me and go before me in order to work in me.

What is the nature of God that you see?

God is the Alpha and Omega. He is the beginning and the end.

What is the kingdom principle you hear?

The Lord goes before us to give us courage and strength. He will never leave us nor forsake us.

Enter *Courage* **into search for inquiry.**

> *Be of good courage, and he shall strengthen your heart, all ye that* **hope** *in the* L$_{ORD}$. *(Psalm 31:24 KJV)*

> God will enable us through the trial and keep us from being fainthearted because we put our trust in him. Hope is having a positive expectation of good in our future. Faith and trust in God is our future. The Lord preserves the faithful.

Worship and thanksgiving prayer

God, you are redemptive. What the enemy means for my harm you will use for good. Thank you that you will go before me and preserve my life. You are my strength and my hope.

Declare truth to receive your treasure:

Jesus Christ is the **door of hope**.

How has your new sight changed your understanding of God?

What do you hear God saying to you?

Journal

Prayer and Community Support

He who dwells in the secret place of the Most High
will rest in the shadow of the Almighty.
—Psalm 91:1 (WEB)

I prayed to God: "I am sheltered in you. I give up my life to you. I put myself in your hands. I submit to your will. I give you all that I am. I am safe because I am in you. I am in you, and you are in me. I am living in the shadow of the Almighty."

> "No weapon that is formed against you shall prosper; and **every tongue that shall rise against you in judgment you shall condemn**. This is the heritage of the servants of Yahweh, and their righteousness which is of me," says Yahweh. (Isaiah 54:17 WEB)

One Sunday, my pastor and my community prayed for me that **no weapon formed against me shall prosper**. They prayed for me to have wisdom and understanding to help me make decisions along the way.

Anytime the Word of God comes, there is warfare. So, **fight for the beauty and treasure of the utterance of God** in the midst of the muck.

New Posture

I became agitated in my spirit regarding my will versus God's will for my life.

In the early morning hours, when I was still half asleep, I was coming in and out with thoughts as though I was in a conversation with God. I was wrestling with coming into a new posture. It was similar to Jacob in his dream about the ladder and the descending and ascending of the angels. I was reminded of Jesus in the garden of Gethsemane as he was in agony, praying, *"Father, if you are willing, remove this cup from me, yet not my will but your will be done."*

I submit to your will. Not my will, but your will be done. That was followed by days when I felt God's love more strongly.

I began to see a pattern of principles to guide me through the journey. In Job I saw that God removed the hedge to demonstrate the development of Job's righteousness. He was blameless and shunned evil and God rewarded him in the end. He also stood in representation for his friends and prayed for them.

Declaration of faith: God, my desire is to dwell in the secret place of your will and find rest in the shadow of your wing. Not my will but your will be done in my life.

❖ Are you willing to submit your life to the will of God?

What is the nature of God that you see?
God is an Almighty God. He is a place of rest and safety.
What is the kingdom principle you hear?
God has given us the authority through Jesus Christ to rise and condemn any judgment the enemy places on us.
Enter *Rise* into search for inquiry.

I rise before dawn and cry for help. I put my hope in your words. (Psalm 119:147 WEB)

But ***I will sing of Your power;*** *yes,* ***I will sing aloud of Your mercy in the morning;*** *for You have been my defense and refuge in the day of my trouble. To You, O my Strength,* ***I will sing praises****; for God is my defense, my God of mercy.* (Psalm 59:16–17 NKJV)

> If you are feeling troubled, begin your day with a song of praise. Play music, and sing along or sing in your heavenly language. Just go with it as the Holy Spirit leads.
>
> ***My soul shall be satisfied as with marrow and fatness; and my mouth shall praise you with joyful lips.*** (Psalm 63:5 NKJV)
>
> Bone marrow is the substance in the hollow part of the bone that produces new blood cells. Healthy marrow is imperative for life. The blood cells transport oxygen to the body and get rid of carbon dioxide, which leaves your body through the lungs when you breathe out. These blood cells also help to stop bleeding and fight against infection.
>
> **Praise** produces health and life to our spirit, soul, and body and acts as an immune system from the cares of the world. Praise invites the presence of God to dwell in you that you might also dwell in the secret place of the Most High God.

Worship and thanksgiving prayer

Heavenly Father, you are an almighty God worthy of praise. You put a song in my heart to honor and worship my Creator. I pray that the fruit of my lips will be a sweet sound to your ears.

Declare truth to receive your treasure:
I will rise to sing of your power, mercy, and might.

My heart sings a song of praise.

How has your new sight changed your understanding of God?
What do you hear God saying to you?

Journal

I Am Weak, but He Is Strong

I already knew that my strongest weapon was to worship God—to give thanks in all things and make a joyful noise unto the Lord. So in order to conquer the fear, there was one thing left to do.

> Finally, **be strong in the Lord, and in the strength of His might.** Put on the whole armor of God that you may be able to stand against the wiles of the devil. (Ephesians 6:10–11 NKJV)

I had to establish in my heart and mind WHOSE strength this is. I had to determine in my mind that his will is of the utmost importance to me. I had to establish that the enemy can be defeated if you put on the entire armor of God.

The Lord is the strength of my life. My concept of death had to change. The armor is a thinking system. It is supernaturally transforming me.

Watson, make your **declaration of faith**:

❖ Do you want to be strong in the Lord?

Enter *Worship* into the search box to do your own word search.

In your journal,

1. record the Scripture and
2. write down what <u>you hear God saying to you</u> about "worship." (This is called a stream of inner transaction with God.) Listen—what truth is God depositing into your heart?

How has your new sight changed your understanding of God?

What do you hear God saying to you?

Journal

Lay It Down

My moment of truth as they say was to make a declaration that **the enemy cannot take my life—I lay it down.** Jesus said that no one takes his life, but he lays it down himself. "I have power to lay it down."

The first part of the process was to bring me to a place of death of my dreams and my personal desires. That repositioned me to be able to hear God correctly. I had to lay it all down to hear the Father's voice, to hear his heart. What is his plan in the earth? What is his desire for mankind?

He had a plan for my life from the beginning. Now it was time to move into a place of identity, maturity, and authority as a son to be about my Father's business. I was in the early stage of understanding, and my compassion for people was increasing along with the ability to look beyond a person's exterior. I was moving into synchronization with God's desires and ways.

Declaration of faith: The enemy cannot take my life. I lay it down for your purpose, Lord.

❖ What is God asking you to lay down?

What is the nature of God that you see?
God is our protector. He covers us with his armor.
What is the kingdom principle you hear?
Put on the whole armor of God. Be strong in the Lord and the power of his might.
Enter *Strength* into search for inquiry.

> For **You have armed me with strength for the battle**; You have subdued under me those who rose up against me. (Psalm 18:39 NKJV)

What a wise Father we have. He strategically allows circumstances to come into our lives to challenge us to grow and mature, but he will not allow us to be overtaken. He will make a way through it where there is no way. He does not send us out into the battle unprepared. He clothes us with his armor.

Most all of us know the story of David and Goliath. It is one of our favorites because it is the little guy against the giant, and David wins against all odds.

This is what David had to say about facing the giant:

Then David said to the Philistine, "You come to me with a sword, with a spear, and with a javelin. But I come to you in the name of the Lord of hosts, the God of the armies of Israel, whom you have defied. This day the Lord will deliver you into my hand, and I will strike you and take your head from you. And this day I will give the carcasses of the camp of the Philistines to the birds of the air and the wild beasts of the earth, that all the earth may know that there is a God in Israel. Then all this assembly shall know that the Lord does not save with sword and spear; **for the battle is the Lord's, and He will give you into our hands**." (1 Samuel 17:45–47)

Worship and thanksgiving prayer

God, you are my strength. The battle is in your hands. I am weak, but you are strong. Thank you for preparing me for the battle. Thank you for giving me your armor, and thank you that the victory belongs to you.

Declare truth to receive your treasure:

The Battle Is the Lord's

How has your new sight changed your understanding of God?

What do you hear God saying to you?

Journal

The Elephant in the Room

Therefore, put on the whole armor of God, that you may be able to withstand in the evil day, and, having done all, to stand.
—Ephesians 6:13 (WEB)

It was time to talk to myself about the most difficult part of the journey for me. I called it the "elephant in the room."

The **"elephant in the room"** is an English metaphorical idiom for an obvious truth that is either being ignored or going unaddressed. The idiomatic expression also applies to an obvious problem or risk no one wants to discuss.

At the surgeon's office, the first thing he asked was "What have you been reading?" He then asked me to tell him what I knew and later asked if I had read the statistics. We didn't discuss it, but I knew what he meant. The statistics are based on the percentage of survivors who live five years after diagnosis.

You think about the "what-ifs." You think about your loved ones and how it might affect their lives, and then there was the dreaded chemotherapy—the poison you put into your body intravenously to kill the cancer, which is accompanied by horrific side effects.

Questions formed in my mind about what course would this take? Some of the next decisions were the following:

- Who do I tell, and when do I tell them?
- How do I tell them?
- How do I find another surgeon?
- Who do I ask to walk with me through it?

Watson, make your **declaration of faith**:

- ❖ Do you have an elephant in your room?
- ❖ Is there something you don't want to talk about?

Enter **Stand** into the search box to do your own word search. I would suggest you look in Psalms and Proverbs.

> In your journal, do the following:
>
> 1. Record the Scripture.
> 2. Write down what <u>you hear God saying to you</u> about "stand." (This is called a stream of inner transaction with God.) Listen—what truth is God depositing into your heart?

How has your new sight changed your understanding of God?

What do you hear God saying to you?

Journal

Drive Away the Vultures

*For though we walk in the flesh, we don't wage war according to the flesh; for the **weapons of our warfare** are not of the flesh, but **mighty before God** to the **throwing down of strongholds, throwing down imaginations and every high thing that is exalted against the knowledge of God**, and **bringing every thought into captivity to the obedience of Christ**.*
—2 Corinthians 10:3–5 (WEB)

I finally located a surgeon who specialized in breast surgery. Her office was in a hospital about eighty miles from where I lived. During the weeks, while I was waiting to hear about an appointment, the enemy swooped in with lies, distortions, sarcasm, and pretense to weaken my resolve and to break my covenant with God to trust him with my life. The enemy began to tell me how insignificant I was in such a vast universe, etc., but God showed me through a small act of kindness that I did for a stranger that no one and no action is insignificant when done in his name.

There is no victory without vigilance. My friend Lizi rode with me to meet the surgeon. While driving on a country road to the hospital, I noticed a vulture, a buzzard, in the middle of the road picking at roadkill. I was driving rather fast and didn't slow down because I expected him to move. Finally, I was almost right upon him and he flew up in front of my windshield and we were eye to eye. Then he vanished. Lizi and I were astonished at the imagery. I had not flinched. I was not shrinking back.

Declaration of faith: I will bring every thought that is exalted against the knowledge of God into captivity to the obedience of Christ.

- ❖ Does the enemy try to make you feel insignificant?
- ❖ Have you determined not to flinch or shrink back?

What is the nature of God that you see?

God is the same yesterday, today, and tomorrow. He is eternal. He does not change. He is a mighty God.

What is the kingdom principle you hear?

After you bring every exalted thought into captivity then stand on the Word of God, what you know to be true.

Enter *Steadfast* into search for inquiry.

> *He (the upright) will not be afraid of evil tidings; His heart is **steadfast**, trusting in the Lord. His heart is established; He will not be afraid.* (Psalm 112:7–8 NKJV)

> The man who walks in the ways of God will not be shaken when he hears bad news. His trust is the Lord because his heart is established in the ways of God.
>
> *You are of God, little children, and have overcome them; because **greater is he who is in you than he who is in the world**.* (1 John 4:4 WEB)

Worship and thanksgiving prayer

God, you are greater than the enemy of this world. Your Word is true, and you are true to your word. I stand on the Word. Thank you that I can trust you to be the same yesterday, today, and tomorrow.

Declare truth to receive your treasure:

I am taking thoughts captive.

>Whatever things are **true**, whatever things are **honorable**, whatever things are **just**, whatever things are **pure**, whatever things are **lovely**, whatever things are **of good report**; if there is any **virtue,** and if there is any **praise**, <u>think about these things</u>. (Philippians 4:8 WEB)

How has your new sight changed your understanding of God?
What do you hear God saying to you?

Journal

Put on the Garment of Praise

To appoint unto them that mourn in Zion, to give unto them a garland for ashes, the oil of joy for mourning, **the garment of praise for the spirit of heaviness;** *that they may be called trees of righteousness, the planting of Jehovah, that he may be glorified.*
—Isaiah 61:3

The night before surgery, I told God that I was offering up to him the sacrifice of praise. "I pray that my sacrifice is a sweet fragrance to you. I thank you for bringing me to this place, building principles in me along the way, and unveiling yourself to me. Thank you for keeping me in the "shadow of your wings."

- ❖ Do you want to put on the garment of praise to change a spirit of heaviness?

Walking through the Storm

Count it all joy, my brothers, when you fall into various temptations *knowing that the testing of your faith produces endurance*. Let endurance have its perfect work that you may be perfect and complete, lacking in nothing.
—James 1:2–4 (WEB)

The surgery went well, but I was at the hospital ten hours, not one and a half like the first surgeon had told me. I returned home and threw up the bright-blue dye used to trace the sentinel lymph node. I healed for six weeks followed by six and a half weeks of radiation.

Six weeks later, my digestive system shut down, and I was unable to eat or drink, which landed me back in the hospital again for another ten days—back on IV prednisone to stop the flare-up and bleeding in my colon.

Two days after I returned home, I was going into the den and turned abruptly to change direction and smashed my toe into the wooden trim around the door. I thought I might have broken it, but by morning, it was fine. However, over the next six weeks, my foot began to swell, and the skin began to slough off as my toe blackened. I went to four doctors and explained to each of them what had happened. None of them gave me any solutions or relief for the pain. Finally, my dear friend Rosie came to my rescue with her wheelchair and took me to the podiatrist. That doctor told me it looked like a spider bite.

Adamantly I said, "<u>No</u>, it is not a spider bite."

Thankfully, he did admit me to the hospital for pain relief. The next morning, his partner prescribed an MRI and returned in the evening to tell me that my toe would need to be amputated and also he would need to remove about four or five inches of the bone in my foot because it was infected. I called my husband to give him the news, feeling relived that that pain would be gone, but it was more than I was expecting.

I had surgery and then went to a long-term acute care (LTAC) facility for wound care, pain management, physical therapy, and three weeks of three different IV antibiotics. It was a Christian-operated LTAC, and the nurses, doctor, and staff were outstanding. I really did feel that God had me in the palm of his hand. I arrived home two weeks before Christmas using a scooter to get around the house for another three weeks.

That had been my year for 2013. When it was all over, God said to me, "**Count it all joy**." There was a part of me that wanted to say, "Really?" But I knew what God was saying. I better understood the Scripture:

> *Let us run with endurance the race that is set before us, looking unto* *Jesus, the author and finisher of our faith**, who* **for the joy that was set before Him endured the cross**. (Hebrews 12:1–2 NKJV)

Jesus had suffered more than I could ever comprehend or imagine, enduring the cross in obedience to the Father and could still count it joy because of his eternal love for you and me. He could see into the future.

Just before Jesus was going to be arrested, he prayed about those things that weighed most heavily in his heart. He prayed to his Father on behalf of his disciples (and you and me), saying,

> Now I come to you, and I say these things in the world **that they may have my joy made full in themselves**…and that **they may all be one**; even as you, Father, are in me, and I in you, that **they also may be one in us**; that the world may believe that you sent me… and **that they may be perfected in unity**… and that they **be with Me where I am** in order that they may behold My glory which You

have given Me, for You did love Me before the foundation of the world.

I had completed the year and returned for a checkup with my primary doctor. He was the doctor who had admitted me into the hospital when I was unable to eat. He knew about the swelling in my foot, but that was all. He walked in and asked how I was doing.

I said, "Well, another domino fell," referring to the sequence of events for the year.

He looked at my foot and could see that my body was worn from the battle. He said, "Can I ask you a question? Are you depressed?"

I didn't understand what he was asking. I realized my body was weary, but my spirit, man, was stronger than ever. I replied, "I don't know, but what I can tell you is that I don't feel like a victim." Then I teared up and said, **"I just don't know if I can find my way back."**

My husband took me home, and I sat down on the couch, thinking that was really an odd thing to say—back to where?

Declaration of faith: God, I count my trials joy because I know the testing of my faith produces endurance. Jesus endured the cross for us so that we might be one with him.

❖ Have you had a trial that produced more endurance?

What is the nature of God that you see?
Jesus is the author and finisher of our faith. Everything originates in him, from him, through him, and is completed in him.

What is the kingdom principle you hear?
The testing of our faith produces endurance. Praise will overcome a spirit of heaviness.

Enter *Endure* into search for inquiry.

For His anger is but for a moment, his favor is for life; weeping may **endure** *for a night, but joy comes in the morning.* (Psalm 30:5 NKJV)

> There is no joy without sorrow. There is no morning without night.
>
> When you have walked through the valley, it makes the mountaintop seem just that much higher.
>
> We need not condemn ourselves for sorrowful choices of the past. The past is the past. Weep and move on. God's favor is for life.
>
> **It is the journey that forges us to make us strong.**

Worship and thanksgiving prayer

God, you are a God of oneness and unity. Thank you for trials that give us endurance to journey into you, into oneness and unity.

Declare truth to receive your treasure:
The testing of my faith builds **endurance**.
God, I ask you for

Endurance **to Persevere to the Finish**

How has your new sight changed your understanding of God?

What do you hear God saying to you?

Journal

The Parables

Then his disciples asked him, "What does this parable mean?" He said, "To you it is given to know the mysteries of the Kingdom of God, but to the rest in parables; that seeing they may not see, and hearing they may not understand."
—Luke 8:9–10

Jesus is saying to you, who are followers, to those who have a desire to know truth and walk in it, I will tell you the secrets of God. The others will see and not see and hear and not understand.

A parable is an earthly story with a heavenly meaning.

I had completed a year of looking into both the earthly realm and the heavenly realm to see the fullness of what God was doing. Now I had more confidence, boldness, and authority to partner with God in a new way.

When we enter a place of more intimacy with God,

> No longer is there any distance between His intent and our ability to understand and act within the framework of that intent. (DNW)

Delight yourself also in the Lord, and He shall give you the desires of your heart. Commit your way to the Lord, trust also in Him, and He shall bring it to pass. (Psalm 37:4–5 NKJV)

To know the heart of God, to know his nature and his ways had always been the desire of my heart. He had revealed more of himself to me because I had committed my way to him and trusted in him. That is partnership—walking in seamless collaboration with his mind.

This led me to pray differently, to pray in confidence "Your kingdom come, your will be done, on earth as it is in heaven." I had positioned myself for battle against all opposing forces of darkness and was now equipped with the finishing spirit of the apostolic mentality partnering with God to open my blind eyes and commit to becoming mature.

Dr. Noel Woodroffe calls this "governmental prayer" and says it is the clearest expression of the warfare of the Apostolic Move of God. It expresses the mentality and the irresistible position of people committed to change in order to be built in the likeness of Christ.

Declaration of faith: I will delight myself in you, God. I will commit my way to you and trust in you.

- ❖ Do you want to know the mysteries of God?
- ❖ Do you commit your way to God?

What is the nature of God that you see?

God knows the desires of our heart and has the power to bring it into reality.

What is the kingdom principle you hear?

Delight in the Lord, commit your way to God and trust in him and he will give you the knowledge and wisdom to know the mystery of the kingdom of God.

Enter *Kingdom of God* into search for inquiry.

> "'You shall **love the Lord your God with all your heart, and with all your soul, and with all your mind, and with all your strength.'** This is the first commandment. The second is like this, **'You shall love your neighbor as yourself.'** There is no other commandment greater than these." The scribe said to him, "Truly, teacher, you have said well that He is one, and there is none other but He, and to love Him with all the heart, and with all the understanding, with all the soul, and with all the strength, and to

love his neighbor as himself, is more important than all whole burnt offerings and sacrifices." When Jesus saw that he answered wisely, he said to him, **"You are not far from the Kingdom of God**.*" No one dared ask him any question after that.* (Mark 12:30–34 WEB)

We don't want to be found among a people of religion that walk the walk and talk the talk but fail to connect with the heart of God.
It must be all of me for all of you, God.

Behold, to obey is better than sacrifice. (1 Samuel 15:22 KJV)

Obedience to the will of God puts an end to religion. It makes rituals and ceremony obsolete.

Not everyone who says to me, "Lord, Lord," will enter into the Kingdom of Heaven; *but* <u>he who does the will of</u> <u>my Father who is in heaven</u>. *Many will tell me in that day, "Lord, Lord, didn't we prophesy in your name, in your name cast out demons, and in your name do many mighty works?"* **Then I will tell them, "I never knew you. Depart from me, you who work iniquity."** (Matthew 7:21–23 WEB)

Worship and thanksgiving prayer

God, you see our hearts, and you say to love you with all our heart, soul, mind, and strength. Thank you, God, for a heart to love you and obey you.

Declare truth to receive your treasure:

It has been given to me to

Know the Mystery
of the Kingdom of God

How has your new sight changed your understanding of God?
What do you hear God saying to you?

Journal

War Cry

***I will praise the name of God with a song, and
will magnify him with thanksgiving.***
—Psalm 69:30

Father, I sing to you a song of joy, blessing, and honor for your faithfulness and loving-kindness throughout my journey.

Take up the whole armor of God

> *Finally, my brethren,* **be strong in the Lord and in the power of His might.** *Put on the whole armor of God that you may be able to stand against the wiles of the devil.* **For we do not wrestle against flesh and blood, but against principalities, against powers, against the rulers of the darkness of this age, against spiritual hosts of wickedness in the heavenly places.** *Therefore,* **take up the whole armor of God** *that you may be able to withstand in the evil day, and having done all, to stand.* (Ephesians 6:10–20)
>
> Stand therefore, having girded your waist with **truth**. (v. 14)

Thank you, God, that you made me to be a seeker of truth. Having put on the breastplate of **righteousness, thank you, God, that Jesus Christ has given me his righteousness.**

> And having shod your feet with the preparation of the gospel of **peace**. (v. 15)

Thank you, God, that you have given me the peace that surpasses all understanding.

> Above all, taking the shield of **faith** with which, you will be able to quench all the fiery darts of the wicked one. (v. 16)

Thank you, God, for giving me the faith that your Word is true and you are true to your Word.

> And take the helmet of **salvation**. (v. 15)

Thank you, God, for your power that has delivered me time and time again, partnered with your redemptive nature.

> And the **sword of the Spirit**, which is the word of God. (v. 17)

Thank you, God, for showing me how to use the **sword of the spirit** to fight and to hear the beauty and treasure of your voice in the midst of the battle.
Thank you, God, for the adverse things in my life that have shaped me to be an overcomer.

> *In Me you may have peace*. In the world you will have tribulation; but be of good cheer, I have overcome the world. (John 16:33 NKJV)

Thank you, Jesus, that you defeated the enemy.
Thank you, God, that you chose me to be conformed to the image of your Son.

> For whom He foreknew, He also predestined to be conformed to the image of His Son,

> *that He might be the firstborn among many brethren.* (Romans 8:29 NKJV)

> *And do not be conformed to this world,* ***but be transformed by the renewing of your mind****.* (Romans 12:2)

Thank you, God, for not allowing the enemy to take my life even though he has tried many times to do so.

> **Have You not made a hedge around him.** (Job 1:10)

> **Only do not lay a hand on his person.** (Job 1:12)

> **And the Lord said to Satan, "Behold, he is in your hand, but spare his life."** (Job 2:6)

Thank you, God, for your strength to go through adversity and finish strong.

> *And He said to me, "My grace is sufficient for you,* **for My strength is made perfect in weakness***."* (2 Corinthians 12:9)

Thank you, God, for sight to see the reality behind the reality.

> You **have made known to me the ways of life;** *You will make me full of joy in Your presence.* **(Acts 2:28)**

> *They sing the song of Moses, the servant of God, and the song of the Lamb, saying: "*Great

> *and marvelous are Your works, Lord God Almighty! Just and true are Your ways."*
(Revelation 15:3)

Thank you, God, for teaching me that my greatest weapons are thanksgiving and worship

> *Rejoice always, pray without ceasing,* **in everything give thanks**; *for this is the will of God in Christ Jesus for you.* (1 Thessalonians 5:16–18)

> *You must worship the L*ord *your God and serve only him.* (Matthew 4:10)

> *But the time is coming—indeed it's here now—when true worshipers will worship the Father in spirit and in truth. The Father is looking for those who will worship him that way.* **For God is Spirit**, *so those who worship him must worship in spirit and in truth.* (John 4:23–24)

Father, this is the song I sing to you from my heart.

*****

I became good friends with a young woman named Karla. She came to America from Trinidad to complete her education in advanced degrees. She developed a relationship with a young man in our community, moved to Texas from Ohio, and they were married. Although Karla was much younger than me, she was a member of a community in Trinidad and had been taught about apostolic grace from an early age by Dr. Noel Woodroffe. Needless to say, she is a strong, godly woman of wisdom and grace.

I sent her an email about what I was experiencing. She replied, "I love the way you included thanking God in your **War Cry**." My response was "Oh, so that is what it is. I didn't know that." **I am a warrior!**

Declaration of faith: God, I will praise your name and magnify you with thanksgiving. I will worship you in spirit and in truth.

❖ Who do you worship? What do you worship?

What is the nature of God that you see?
God is spirit. His works are great and marvelous, and his ways are just and true. He is a God of peace.

What is the kingdom principle you hear?
Those who worship God must worship him in spirit and in truth.

Be strong in the Lord and in the power of his might.

We do not wrestle against flesh and blood but against principalities, against powers, against the rulers of the darkness of this age, against spiritual hosts of wickedness in the heavenly places.

Be transformed by the renewing of your mind.

Worship the Lord your God, and serve only him.

Enter *Worship* into search for inquiry.

> He (Satan) said to him, *"I will give you all of these things, if you will fall down and worship me."* Then Jesus said to him, *"Get behind me, Satan! For it is written, 'You shall worship the Lord your God, and him only shall you serve.'"* (Matthew 4:9–10 WEB)

One definition of *worship* is a valuing or a treasuring of God above all things. I like that

> definition because this is a book about seeking treasures of wisdom and knowledge. We will pursue that which we treasure.
>
> Worship is a heart issue. It is a lifestyle and a lifelong pursuit. If you do not pursue God, then you will pursue something else not of God.
>
> Satan tempted Jesus with all Satan had to offer if only Jesus would worship him. He makes us the same offer today.
>
> Jesus responded, *"Get behind me, Satan! For it is written, 'You shall worship the Lord your God, and him only shall you serve.'"*

Worship and thanksgiving prayer

God, I will pursue you with all my heart, mind, and soul. I thank you for the power of your might to overcome the temptations of the world.

Declare truth to receive your treasure:

Be strong in the **power of his might**.

How has your new sight changed your understanding of God?

What do you hear God saying to you?

Journal

Functional Sonship Is Our True Identity

I prayed for the revelation of the "Spirit" of sonship. The voice of God tells me who I am. I made a commitment to continue to track maturity in my life. **It is impossible to advance without an offering of sacrifice and death to self.**

The beginning of wisdom is **acquire wisdom; and with all your acquiring, get understanding. Watch over your heart with all diligence, for from it flows the springs of life.**

> Then the Lord said to Satan, "Have you considered My servant Job, that there is none like him on the earth, a **blameless and upright man, one who fears God and shuns evil**?" (Job 1:8 NKJV)

God removed the hedge of protection which he had placed around Job and allowed Satan to test him. "Then you will see the development of my son—a singular standard." Job was tested and did not sin. My heart's cry is "God, show me what you want me to know about you. Who do you want me to become?"

He said that he wants to release all those who are imprisoned and oppressed in Babylon. "You are my weapon."

> You are My war club (battle axe) My weapon for battle—**with you I shatter nations, with you I destroy kingdoms**. (Jeremiah 51:20 NIV)

God was telling me that he was using me but I also was in partnership with him. My church community and other communities around the world were tracking final maturity in their lives just as I had been doing. We had become an army of warriors.

> We are the body of Christ praying ultimate prayers that cause the written prophetic purposes of God to be fulfilled. (DNW)

In the Old Testament, God had made a blood covenant with Israel to deliver them out of bondage, which foreshadowed the covenant of the Savior of Jesus Christ to deliver us.

> *As for you also, Because of the **blood of your covenant**, I have set free your prisoners from the pit in which is no water. Turn to the **stronghold**, you prisoners of hope! Even today I declare that I will restore double to you. (Zechariah 9:11–12 WEB)*

Today people are imprisoned in spiritually "waterless places." They are trapped without hope, journey, or revelation. God is breaking the oppression over his people and releasing them to a place of hope.

But in order for me to be in partnership to set others free, I had to be freed first from the stronghold that the enemy had on my life.

Watson, make your **declaration of faith**:

- ❖ Do you want to be set free from a spiritual waterless place?
- ❖ Do you want to turn to the stronghold of hope?

Enter *Wisdom* into the search box to do your own word search. I would suggest you look in Psalms and Proverbs.

In your journal, do the following:

1. Record the Scripture.
2. Write down what <u>you hear God saying to you</u> about "wisdom." (This is called a stream of inner transaction with God.) Listen—what truth is God depositing into your heart?

Loving with a Whole Heart

Jesus said to him, "You shall love the Lord your God with all your heart, and with all your soul, and with all your mind."
—Matthew 22:37 (WEB)

Some time passed, and I was healing from the surgeries, but the flare-ups and bleeding in my colon continued. I had now battled ulcerative colitis for about forty years. The doctor said, "We don't see many like you." I had resisted having an ileostomy, the surgery to have my colon and rectum removed.

When I was about nine years old, my uncle had had this type of surgery because he had suffered also with ulcerative colitis. I remembered the family talking about it, and I thought at the time that that was something I would never, never want to happen to me. I tried everything I knew to make the disease better. I had radically altered my diet to eliminate inflammatory foods. I took food supplements. I tried a variety of medications, and I was always on the hunt for something new.

One day, God said, **"You have not given me your whole heart. You have withheld a part of your heart from me."** I thought about it and realized he was talking about my colon. I had prayed. My pastor had prayed. I think about everyone I knew had prayed for my healing. I was hoping and hoping I would not have to have surgery. This is what I never, never wanted to happen.

But in my heart, I knew God was right. That was the part of my heart that I had withheld from him, so, I prayed and told him that he could have that part too. He could have my colon.

The bouts of bleeding became more frequent, and my body began to scream, "No more prednisone." I had the surgery in January 2016, and it was everything I thought it would be. God sent my sister and daughter to be my advocates at the hospital. He knew in his mercy that I would need them. They stayed with me day and night for three days. Barely conscious and in horrific pain, the doctor said he would send me home in five days. Once again, God intervened. My daughter located a facility nearby where I could go for care; however, they were having complications with the paperwork. Meanwhile I began to have some infection, and the doctor took out most of the staples to open the incision running vertically down my belly to let it drain. They stuffed my belly with gauze, and I remained in the hospital for two weeks. It took five months for the incision to fully close, and then there was the dreaded pouch stuck on my belly for the rest of my life. As you can ascertain, I still wasn't pleased about the idea.

It has been almost seven years now, and the question to ask is "How is God working it for good?" I told a friend the other day it forces me to **choose every day** between living according to my flesh or choosing to die to self and worship God in the midst of it.

It is a constant **reminder of my journey with God** and his faithfulness to give me the desire of my heart, which is to know his heart. It is a **reminder to me not to shrink back** but fight on to the finish of his plan and his desire.

It reminds me every day of Christ's love for his body and his ultimate sacrifice on the cross for you and me. It reminds me of his final prayer to God expressing his heart's cry just prior to going back to heaven to sit at the right hand of God.

It reminds me every day that Christ is asking me to love the body of Christ and **be the watchman on the wall** for others as he leads us all out of the bondage of this fallen world system.

Declaration of faith: God, I will love you with all my heart, my soul, and my mind.

- ❖ Have you withheld a part of your heart from God?
- ❖ Is there something you have told him that you never want to happen to you?

What is the nature of God that you see?
God is a God of covenant. He is our stronghold.

What is the kingdom principle you hear?

Acquire wisdom, and get understanding. Watch over your heart with all diligence. Love the Lord your God with all your heart and with all your soul and with your entire mind.

Enter *Diligence* **into search for inquiry.**

> *We desire that each one of you may show the same* diligence **to the fullness of hope even to the end**, *that you won't be sluggish, but imitators of those who through faith and patience inherited the promises.* (Hebrews 6:11–12 WEB)

Diligent to

1. have fullness of hope to the end,
2. not be sluggish,
3. imitate those who through faith and patience inherit the promise of God.

We are to acquire wisdom and understanding as we journey through the trials but keep pressing forward with diligence, continuing in the fullness of hope.

I had journeyed through the storm, acquiring wisdom and understanding, but what comes next? It is faith and patience to see the reality of the fruit of the journey. Remember, God said if we delight in him, he will give us the desires of our heart. That is a promise.

Worship and thanksgiving prayer

I worship you, Lord. You are a God of covenant. You are my stronghold in times of trouble. I thank you that you are faithful to the end. Thank you for giving me wisdom and understanding.

Declare truth to receive your treasure:
I will have faith and patience to

Inherit the Promises of God

How has your new sight changed your understanding of God?

What do you hear God saying to you?

Journal

The Key of David

To the angel of the church in Philadelphia write: These are the words of Him who is **holy and true**, *who* <u>**holds the key of David**</u>. *What he opens no one can shut, and what he shuts no one can open. I know your deeds. See, I have placed before you an open door that no one can shut* (Access). *I know that you have little strength, yet you have kept my word and have not denied my name.*
—Revelation 3:7–8

After I had written my "War Cry," God said to ask him for the "key of David." I knew about that because God had put it on my radar many years before, but now Dr. Woodroffe was talking about it.

He explained that it is God who has to permit access to his mind and his plans. God has to open a portal of permission into his mind that cannot be shut by the enemy, whose greatest desire is that we have no access to direction from our Commander above!

> The **key of David is the right of unstoppable access** and is a thing of great value and power. Once applied, it gives access that no power of darkness can prevent. (DNW)

Isaiah 22:20–23 tells us about a servant to the house of David whose name was Eliakim. God says he will lay the key of the house of David on his shoulder

> So **he** shall open, and no one shall shut;
> and **he** shall shut, and no one shall open.

This was my opportunity for partnership, access, alignment, harmony, information, and knowledge of God—all the things I had declared as I entered into my journey through breast cancer.

Could it be true? Could I really have seamless uninterrupted collaboration with the mind of God?

I prayed and asked God to give me the key of David, the spiritual technology to open access to God.

Declaration of faith: God, I ask you for the key of David to have seamless uninterrupted collaboration with your mind.

- ❖ Do you want access to the mind of God?
- ❖ Do you want seamless uninterrupted collaboration with God?

What is the nature of God that you see?

God is holy and true. What he opens no one can shut, and what he shuts no one can open. He knows our deeds.

What is the kingdom principle you hear?

God says he knows our deeds. He is the one who determines to whom he will give access to his mind. He says if we keep his Word and do not deny his name, he will place an open door before us that no one can shut.

Enter *Open* into search for inquiry.

> *The Lord upholds all who fall and raises up all who are bowed down. The eyes of all look expectantly to You, and You give them their food in due season.* **You *open* Your hand and satisfy the desire of every living thing**. (Psalm 145:14–16 NKJV)

> It is only God who can **open** his hand to satisfy the deepest longing of our soul. We look expectantly to him to supply us daily

> with spiritual food and in due season to keep his promise.
>
> God "raises up all who are bowed down."
>
> He exalts the humble. He lifts them up, guides and teaches them, gives them wisdom and honor, and increases their joy in the Lord.

Worship and thanksgiving prayer

God, you are the one that satisfies my soul. You open doors that no one can shut. Thank you for access to your mind to collaborate in partnership with you to do your will in the earth.

Declare truth to receive your treasure:
Thank you for your grace to hold

The Key of David

How has your new sight changed your understanding of God?
What do you hear God saying to you?

Journal

Kingdom of God

I will give to you the keys of the Kingdom of Heaven, and whatever you bind on earth will have been bound in heaven; and whatever you release on earth will have been released in heaven.
—Matthew 16:19 (WEB)

The kingdom of God was a mystery to the men and women who lived during the time of Jesus. The Jews wanted the Messiah to come as the conquering king and save them from the oppression of the Roman Empire, but Jesus said, **"My kingdom is not of this world."**

The kingdom is the sowing of good seed.

> *Then the King will tell those on his right hand, "Come, blessed of my Father, **inherit the Kingdom prepared for you from the foundation of the world**." (Matthew 25:34 WEB)*

> *Jesus answered him, "Most assuredly, I tell you, unless one is born anew, he can't **see** the Kingdom of God." foundation of the world… Jesus answered, "Most assuredly I tell you, unless one is born of water and spirit, he can't **enter** into the Kingdom of God!" (John 3:3, 5 WEB)*

> *Who delivered us out of the power of darkness, and **translated** us into the Kingdom of the Son of his love. (Colossians 1:13 WEB)*

> *And the Lord **will deliver** me from every evil work, and will preserve me for his heavenly Kingdom; to whom be the glory forever and ever. Amen. (2 Timothy 4:18 WEB)*

> Therefore, **_receiving_** a Kingdom that can't be shaken, let us have grace, through which we serve God acceptably, with reverence and awe. (Hebrews 12:28 WEB)

> For thus will be richly supplied to you the **_entrance_** into the eternal Kingdom of our Lord and Savior, Jesus Christ. (Hebrews 12:28 WEB)

> The seventh angel sounded, and great voices in heaven followed, saying, "The kingdom of the world has **_become_** the Kingdom of our Lord, and of his Christ. He will reign forever and ever!" (Revelation 11:15 WEB)

> I heard a loud voice in heaven, saying, "**_Now is come_** the salvation, the power, and the Kingdom of our God, and the authority of his Christ; for the accuser of our brothers has been thrown down, who accuses them before our God day and night." (Revelation 12:10 WEB)

We can see a thread from the promise of our inheritance to seeing, to being born again to enter, to being transformed, to being delivered, to receiving, to allowing entrance, to becoming, to now is salvation come.

Jesus told us to pray to the Father, **"Your kingdom come, your will be done on earth as it is in heaven."**

This pathway existed in Jesus Christ before the foundation of this world, before God even created earth and mankind.

I began thinking about the kingdom of God last night after writing with regards to the key of David. I thought I remembered something Jesus had said about the kingdom. I looked with the help of the concordance; I looked through the topical dictionaries, and I could not find it. I became frustrated and tired and went to sleep.

Later that night, God dropped a word into my spirit. He said, "I Am Healing!" Later in the night, he said, "They Must Match."

So this morning, I began the process of inquiry. "Father, what does that mean? What an odd thing to say." Then I remembered the verse in the Bible where God said to Moses, "I Am Who I Am," and he said, "You shall tell the children of Israel this: **I Am has sent me to you**." Moses was chosen by God to lead the children of Israel out of the bondage of Egypt (Babylon) to the Promised Land.

I Am sent Jesus to earth to be our deliverer from the bondage of a thinking system devised by the enemy. Just before coming in the room to continue my writing, my husband and I were preparing to eat lunch. Max, our cat, jumped to his usual location on the counter to say, "I want you to give me a treat." He has continual access to his bowl of dried cat food but sometimes anticipates my giving him a treat from the food I am eating. I leaned close to his little face, scratching both sides of his head with my fingers, and said, "Yes, if I control your mind, I control your body."

That is what the enemy says to us. The seed sown into the heart grows to become a thinking system to control the body. Therefore, the battle takes place in the mind. The battle is for our soul.

Declaration of faith: God, move me along the pathway of the kingdom of heaven as I journey deeper into you.

❖ Do you desire to be journeying on this pathway?

What is the nature of God that you see?
God is the great I Am. He is the origin of all life.
What is the kingdom principle you hear?
The kingdom in heaven is to match the kingdom in the heart of man.

> **The decrees of God originate in heaven and then flow into the earth.**

Enter *Promise* into the search box to do your own word search. I would suggest you look in Psalms and Proverbs.

> In your journal, do the following:
>
> 1. Record the Scripture.
> 2. Write down what <u>you hear God saying to you</u> about "promise." (This is called a stream of inner transaction with God.) Listen—what truth is God depositing into your heart?

How has your new sight changed your understanding of God?
What do you hear God saying to you?

Journal

They Must Match

Enter in by the narrow gate; for wide is the gate and broad is the way that leads to destruction, and many are those who enter in by it. How narrow is the gate, and **restricted is the way that leads to life**! *Few are those who find it.*
—Matthew 7:13–14 (WEB)

God says, "I am the Alpha and the Omega, the First and the Last, the Beginning and the End." All life originates IN HIM and is sent from him "to become" and return back to him at the completion of his plan and purpose.

Jesus tells the story about ten lepers who had asked for mercy and were healed by faith through their obedience to show themselves to the priest.

One of them, when he saw that he was healed, turned back, glorifying God with a loud voice. He fell on his face at Jesus's feet, giving him thanks, and he was a Samaritan. Jesus asked, "Where are the other nine who were healed? Were there none found **who returned to give glory to God**, except this stranger?"

Then the Pharisees, having a wrong motive and a wrong heart position, asked Jesus, "When would the kingdom of God come?"

Jesus said, "You will not see the kingdom by external observation"—meaning not with pomp and splendor. Once again, he had rebuked the Pharisees for their blindness but then seized the opportunity to speak truth to his disciples.

He answered them by saying,

> The Kingdom of God doesn't come with observation; neither will they say, "Look, here!" or, "Look, there!" for behold, **the Kingdom of God is within you**. (Luke 17:20 WEB)

*Jesus said to him, "**I am the way, the truth, and the life. No one comes to the Father, except through me**." (John 14:6 WEB)*

God is saying, "**Return to me.**"
Jesus is saying, "**Follow me.**"
"I will give you the hidden treasures of the kingdom!"
Then I could see that **I am in the kingdom of heaven, and in the earth, I am the kingdom!**

The challenge

Watson, are you ready? This is your biggest challenge yet.

1. Do you see the kingdom in you? Do you believe God is strengthening your core? How?

Write your own "War Cry," making declarations and giving thanks to God. Review each step along the path beginning with "Faith for the Journey" and move through the list until "Loving with a Whole Heart."

2. Where are you in the kingdom? What is your location?

Review the pathway of the kingdom from "see" to "now is come" and decide where you think you are standing on that pathway. Write it down.

Write answers here:

Whew, well done, Watson!

Now you may collect your reward and move on to the next mountain.

Your reward is as follows:

Shod your feet with the Gospel of peace

Watson, bring along the treasures and your armor.
We will travel on the kingdom pathway to the next mountain.

VI

Knitting Our Hearts Together

*That their **hearts may be comforted, they being knit together in love,** and gaining all riches of the full assurance of understanding, that they may know the mystery of God, both of the Father and of Christ.*
—Colossians 2:2 WEB

Jesus said that the Father is in him and he is in the Father and prayed that believers may also be in them "that we may be **perfected in unity.**"

Jesus Christ is the same yesterday, today, and forever. God exists outside of time.

> *Now may the God who gives perseverance and encouragement grant you to **be of the same mind with one another** according to Christ Jesus that with one accord you may **with one voice glorify** the God and Father of our Lord Jesus Christ.* (Romans 15:5–6 NAS)

The kingdom in earth must match the kingdom in heaven being of the same mind with one voice worshipping God. To knit together is to have interlocking loops. One cannot be separated from the other.

When I was in high school, I was part of a girl's chorus. My senior year, we went to the New York world's fair to sing in the Texas Pavilion. I was one of five girls on a dance team which performed a little choreographed tap dance to a couple of the songs. We all wore shirtwaist dresses of different pastel colors with matching cardigan sweaters. My dress color was lavender, but I was not able to find a matching sweater in the store, so I decided to venture forth to knit my own.

That was my first experience about learning the difference between a knitted fabric and a woven fabric. The properties of woven fabrics differ greatly to properties of knitted fabrics where one is made up of woven wefts and warps; the other is made by looping them. This difference in construction gives both fabric types a completely different characteristic.

Many knit fabrics have the ability to <u>stretch with elasticity and equally</u> <u>good recoverability</u>. When you scrunch a knit textile in your hands, it will ball up easily; and when you release it, it will <u>spring back into shape</u> with hardly any wrinkles.

It is <u>comfortable and breathable</u> and comes in a variety of weights and designs, and it is renowned for standing up to physical activity. It is comfortable to wear and <u>resistant to wrinkling</u>.

I found just the opposite to be true about woven fabrics. My senior year in college, I took a weaving class using a loom. I learned about the **warp** yarn, which is the lateral thread-held stationary in tension on the loom while the **weft** is the horizontal thread drawn through and inserted over and under the warp. A woven fabric is any fabric made by interlacing two or more threads at <u>right angles to one another</u>.

Each warp fiber passes alternately under and over each weft fiber. The fabric is <u>symmetrical,</u> with good *stability* and reasonable penetrability. However, it is the most difficult of the weaves to drape, and the <u>high level of fiber crimp</u> imparts relatively <u>low mechanical properties</u>.

About now, you may be asking, "What does this have to do with knitting our hearts together?" Shortly we will be discussing patterns in our lives. Remember, there are two systems at work in us—the world system designed by Satan (Babylon) and the kingdom of God which Jesus said is within us.

God says our hearts are to be comforted being knit together not woven together. We will explore the difference between the two in this section of the book.

Equipping the Saints

Every writing inspired by God is profitable for teaching, for reproof, for correction, and for instruction which is in righteousness, **that the man of God may be complete, thoroughly equipped for every good work.**
—2 Timothy 3:16 (WEB)

Now **you are the body of Christ**, and members individually. God has set some in the assembly: **first apostles, second prophets, third teachers,** then miracle workers, then gifts of healings, helps, governments, and various kinds of languages.
—1 Corinthians 12:27–28 (WEB)

God establishes rank and order of first apostles, second prophets, and third teachers. Paul identifies himself as an apostle of Jesus Christ by the will of God. He says he is a wise master builder who laid the foundation and another builds on it. If anyone's work which he has built on it endures, he will receive a reward.

But to each one of **us was the grace given according to the measure of the gift of Christ.** (Ephesians 4:7 WEB)

The apostle John said **that from the fullness of Christ Jesus, we all received grace upon grace**. God says "I Am," which means that everything we require for life is in him, but then the question is "How do we access that resource?" So God made a way though Jesus Christ for us to access anything and everything we lack for life.

The Word became flesh, and lived among us. We saw his glory, such glory as of the one and

> *only Son of the Father, **full of grace and truth**.* (John 1:14 (WEB)

Jesus said, "I came that you might have life and have it more abundantly."

> *To me, the very least of all saints, was this grace given, to preach to the Gentiles the unsearchable riches of Christ, and **to make all men see** what is the administration of **the mystery which for ages has been hidden in God**, who created all things through Jesus Christ.* (Ephesians 3:8–9 WEB)

The Word says **God gives grace to the humble**. There is an abundance of it. We access grace through faith in Jesus Christ.

We are to continue in the grace of God, be saved through the grace, believe through the grace, built through the grace to receive an inheritance, and we are justified by grace. **We are joint heirs of the grace of life.**

Grace is given, bestowed on us as a gift. It must reign in us through righteousness to eternal life.

We are under grace; we behave ourselves in the world so that others may abound in this grace.

The riches of **God's grace are sufficient** for us in any circumstance. It is his power made perfect in our weakness. We are to be strengthened in our spirit by grace. **Our heart is to be established by grace.**

Grace is kindness; we are all partakers of the **grace which gives us eternal hope and comfort. Our speech is to be always seasoned with grace.**

We are **called by grace** to a holy calling according to his purpose, which was given to us in Christ Jesus from before the foundation of the world.

We are to be good **stewards of the grace** of God in its various forms and stand in the true grace of God.

We are to draw near with boldness to the throne of grace that we may receive mercy and may **find grace for help in time of need**.

Grace is the power that works in us to do exceedingly abundantly above all we could ask or think in prayer to our Father.

The last verse in the Bible says **the grace of the Lord Jesus Christ be with all the saints. Amen.**

Declaration of faith: God, I ask for the gift of grace that I may be complete and equipped for every good work. I ask for grace upon grace to be a good steward of grace so that others may abound in grace.

❖ Do you desire to have the grace of God?

What is the nature of God that you see?
Jesus Christ is the fullness of grace and truth.
What is the kingdom principle you hear?
The grace that is on us is for others to equip the saints for every good work.
Enter *Mystery* into search for inquiry.

> The **mystery** which has been hidden for ages and generations. But now it has been revealed to his saints, to whom God was pleased to make known what are the riches of the glory of this mystery among the Gentiles, which is Christ in you, the hope of glory. (Colossians 1:26–27 WEB)

> A **mystery** of God is a truth which is undiscoverable except by revelation, long hid but now made manifest.
>
> God is revealing himself to us more and more as we come closer to the finish of his plan in the earth. We have been finding hidden treasures of wisdom and knowledge—Christ in us. It is our hope to manifest Christ in the earth. It is the grace of God to do so.
>
> The mystery was first made known to the disciples and later revealed by the apostle Paul to the Gentiles (non-Jews).
>
> It is made manifest in man as it pleases God to do so. Christ was the fullness of grace. It is given to us grace upon grace, one grace at a time.

Worship and thanksgiving prayer

Father God, how wonderful and astonishing it is that it pleases you to give us grace and reveal the mystery of the riches of the glory of Christ. Thank you that our hearts are established by grace.

Declare truth to receive your treasure:
We are joint heirs with Christ.

 **Grace**

How has your new sight changed your understanding of God?
What do you hear God saying to you?

Journal

A Teaching Dimension

When I had completed (or thought I had) writing the book, I sent a copy to Lizi, my friend who had journeyed with me through cancer and who had encouraged me to journal and track my journey five years earlier. I told her that I was aware it needed editing and formatting, etc., but it also lacks a teaching dimension. I said, "I am not sure if it is part of the book or if it will come alongside of the book in the form of a workbook."

Then God said to me, "You are not done yet. I want you to bring the journey up to date into the current move of God into the prophetic grace." So I quickly sent her an email and said, "Correction—it is not finished yet."

Pivot on the core

In the last section, we focused on strengthening your core. Now we are going to look at what it means to **pivot on the core**. We will explore the walking in the prophetic joined at the heart verses walking in learned established patterns of thinking and behavior.

Have you ever heard the expression "the fabric of our lives"? It refers to our journey through the formative years of our life to shape us by our emotions and feelings which create a perception and philosophy of life. Think of it as a woven fabric. The warp threads of longitude are set in place while the weft threads weave through them in and out to form a pattern.

The warp may be our place of birth, our culture, race, socio-economic position, our family, etc.—the structure of our life in which we have been placed. The weft threads are the events and circumstances that happened to us, causing an emotional reaction and woundedness in our heart. Unbeknown to us, we allow fear to get in our way. We keep ourselves at bay from our own feelings and create a safe distance with others forming a pattern of thinking and behavior. This forms a narrowing of our thinking and right-angled reactions of self-preservation. This is a mechanical process from the outside in.

The opposite is a knitted fabric shaped from the inside out. The yarn is one piece looped in and out with another from beginning to finish. This represents the joining of our heart to Christ. When we invited him into our heart for the first time, it meant he was there to walk with us through thick and thin into the finish. This is a shaping from inside out. To pivot on our core is to respond to life situations from kingdom values and principles rather than emotion.

Our set patterns are in opposition to hearing the voice of God because they have been shaped through fear and disappointment and dissolution. The good times are also part of forming that pattern. We have decided what makes us feel good and bring us comfort in the world.

I asked God about adding a teaching dimension, and immediately I thought about Denise, who is the lead teacher of my home group. Once a month our church meets in small designated groups in someone's home—men with men and women with women. We come together to discuss how we are applying the present apostolic instruction in our daily life.

Denise had been a high school English teacher and had just taken a sabbatical. I asked her to think about adding a teaching dimension. When I checked back with her after a week or so, she said that she had read some of the book but didn't understand what I was asking her to do. I replied, "I am not sure either. Let's spend an afternoon together and discuss it."

The Parable of the Fig Tree

*In the morning, as Jesus was returning to Jerusalem, he was hungry, and he noticed a fig tree beside the road. He went over to see if there were any figs, but there were only leaves. Then he said to it, "May you never bear fruit again!" And immediately the fig tree withered up. The disciples were amazed when they saw this and asked, "How did the fig tree wither so quickly?" Then Jesus told them, "I tell you the truth**, if you have faith and don't doubt, you can do things like this and much more. You can even say to this mountain, 'May you be lifted up and thrown into the sea,' and it will happen. You can pray for anything, and if you have faith, you will receive it**."*
—Matthew 21:18–22 NLT

Watson, first I am going to walk you through the prophetic dimension of Christ. That means to hear what God is saying and to obey and walk in it. God had a plan for Denise and me that day, but we had to discover what it was.

> It is the glory of God to conceal a matter,
> But the glory of kings is to search out a matter.
> (Proverbs 25:2 NKJV)

So Denise and I had set our hearts to search out the matter on the heart of the king of the kingdom.

A pattern of resistance: Denise had some hesitations on deciding to do this.

I live in the country about thirty minutes from her house, so I gave her the choice of my going there or her coming here. She was undecided, so while her husband was standing there, I asked him, "What do you think is best?" He said it would be better for her to leave her surroundings and come to my home in the country. He was implying that he thought there would be less distraction at my house than hers. We chose a day and time and I left.

So I called a week later on the appointed day and asked if she was still planning to come. She was still asking if she was coming to my house or was I coming there. I said, "Yes, you are coming here."

*****

When she arrived, she put her computer and papers on the table, and I said, "Let's go outside. It is a lovely day." I led her to the table on the corner of the surrounding porch of our log home. The view looks out on 110 acres of our farm/ranch.

God steps in with a prophetic sign:

She sat down, opened her laptop computer, and began talking about some editing. While she was talking, I noticed two ripe figs side by side touching each other hanging on the

branch of the large fig tree behind her. I explained, "Oh my gosh! Look, Denise, there are two ripe figs on the tree." The season for figs ended four months ago. Immediately we both thought about the parable of Jesus and the Fig Tree. Why did my tree have figs on it when it was not the season to do so?

Okay, raise your hand if you have never understood that parable. I'm raising mine. It had always been a mystery to me. Denise excitedly said, "Take a picture!" So I went looking for my camera, came back, and took a picture. Seeing the figs inspired me to believe that God wanted to reveal more, so I asked if she would like to take a four-wheeler ride through the property. This was something I was accustomed to doing for many years with the grandchildren.

I set out in faith just moving about as I felt led to do so:

We drove to the barn, hopped on the four-wheeled ATV, and headed out, Denise sitting behind me. The property is divided into pastures bordered by high wire fences to protect the animals and birds. Leading from the house to the barn, we have a pasture for our free-range chickens, on the right a pasture to grow hay for the cattle, on the left a pasture for our milk cows so they have access to the barn area.

As you leave the barn, there is a turkey house and pasture on the right; on the left is a catfish pond and pasture for our pet deer, Ginger, where she would stay while raising her newborn fawns.

We entered through the gate, traveling the lane to explore the remaining seventy acres of heavily wooded pastures. I veered off to a clearing on the left and stopped in front of a five-foot-high mound of dirt and said, "We lost our beloved Ginger last week. Jerry buried her here and carved a cross in the tree to mark the spot. I explained that Jerry had found Ginger thirteen years ago in the high grass while mowing the pasture by our house. We watched over her, but the mother did not return, so we took her into our house. A mother deer will hide her fawn in high grass in a clearing after the fawn is born. Somehow, she communicates to them not to leave the spot. She comes to the fawn at the time of feeding only. From a distance, she stays on watch to lead a predator in chase away from the fawn if needed. Ginger was a great mom and a fierce warrior when protecting her young. She had already been seriously injured once while trying to protect her three young fawns.

Everyone who visited the farm wanted to see Ginger and pet her. She was very friendly. Jerry and Ginger were best buddies. She began her life in our home and sometimes would lie down with our puppies while we watched TV. As she grew older, Jerry built a habitat to accommodate her need. They often walked through the woods with her running a distance ahead and then waiting for him to catch up.

It was their pattern every evening at dusk for Jerry to take her a treat of kernels of corn. He also added protein pellets for her health, which she didn't like nearly as much, but I think she trusted him to know best.

Last week, she did not show up for her treat for a couple of days, and Jerry became suspicious and went looking for her. He found her remains. Her body had been eaten by coyotes and only her carcass and legs remained. We still don't know if she was killed protecting Daisy, her young fawn, or if she died of old age and was eaten afterward. Daisy was one of the last two fawns born to Ginger. She was the runt of the two, and Jerry took her and bottle fed her until she was healthy enough to be returned to Ginger.

As I drove along the lane, I looked at the pasture on the right and said, "I would like to show you that one, but I do not have permission to go in there because of the potential danger." That is the deer pasture and Romeo and the herd are in there. Romeo was another deer that Jerry had raised but was a male. He had crawled up to Jerry's feet one day when Jerry was out building a fence. He was barely alive, and Jerry took him and nursed him back to health. Being a male, he did not have the same disposition as Ginger. I explained to Denise that "It is the breeding season now, and Romeo has a full rack of antlers with ten points. In other words, he is a mature buck. He thinks of Jerry as competition during this season and might challenge him if he enters the pasture."

The Secret Place

O my dove, in the clefts of the rock, **in the secret place of the steep pathway**, *Let me see your countenance, Let me hear voice; For your voice is sweet, and your form is lovely.*
—Song of Solomon 2:14 (NASV)

"Dove" refers to one of beauty with a gentle and peaceful nature. God uses it here as a term of endearment spoken by Christ to the church, his bride.

"Cleft" is a space in the rock formed by a splitting open, a fissure formed over a very long period of time.

The secret place is a place of intimacy with God. It is the place where two become one, the place where hearts are joined, and the mind of God touches down into the heart of the believer.

*****

Upon entering through the gate, I told Denise that we would begin our journey at **"the secret place."** That is the place where my young granddaughter always wanted to go first. She would ask me, "Which way to the secret place, Grammy"? We shut the gate to the cattle pasture and proceeded forward.

I explained to Denise that the land looked different now than it did when we bought the property sixteen years ago. Originally the back side was so dense with trees and underbrush that you could not travel through it. The property also had deep gullies where the water traversed the land, eroding the soil.

On weekends Jerry drove his tractor into the woods, knocking down small trees and clearing under bush to open trails through the woods. Where needed, he also put in culverts to form a passageway for the water to run under the trails.

The secret place is the deepest part of the property. The steep decline into the ravine and the steep ascent on the other side out of the ravine is paved with an array of multicolored stones. The smooth surface of the stones is the result of water washing over them for hundreds, maybe thousands of years, as they became exposed over time. Also one might find scattered treasures of petrified wood ranging in size from small to large. That part remains the same.

However, the bottom is greatly changed. It used to be a wonderland of green moss clinging to parts of the large trees accompanied by grey moss dangling downward two to three feet from the branches. When it rained, it formed a creek crossing through it which traveled into the woods. Both my granddaughters loved to hunt for the few chosen stones to put into the rock polisher to be tumbled and shine forth their beauty. Meanwhile, I searched for my treasures of petrified wood to take back to the house and put in my garden, but the most enjoyable part was cutting the hanging grapevine entangled in the trees loose from the thorny vines which held them captive. My granddaughter and I would take the big clippers with us and cut them loose, saying, "I set you free." One time we took the tender green grapevine back to the house and shaped it to become a wreath for Racheal's bedroom. When we were done, we held it up to look at it and discovered it had taken the shape of a heart.

If you look at the imagery of this place, it represents the way and privilege of access to the presence of God. It is filled with treasures which were once hidden but have now become exposed. The stream represents the water of life that flows from the throne of God.

The rigid thorny vine growing upward out of the ground represents the entanglement of our mentalities with the world, but when it is cut free by the salvation of Christ, the grapevine dangles freely before our face, yielding the fruit of right living, and the vine is accessible to be reached and shaped into God's purpose for our life.

One of the places in the Bible where you see the knitting of hearts together in love is John 12:1–7 (NKJV):

> Then, six days before the Passover, Jesus came to Bethany, where Lazarus was who had been dead, whom He had raised from the dead. There they made Him a supper; and Martha served, but Lazarus was one of those who sat at the table with Him. **Then Mary took a pound of very costly oil of spikenard, anointed the feet of Jesus, and wiped His feet with her hair.** And the house was filled with the fragrance of the oil.
> But one of His disciples, Judas Iscariot, Simon's son, who would betray Him, said, "Why was this fragrant oil not sold for three hundred denarii and given to the poor?" This he said, not that he cared for the poor, but because he was a thief, and had the money box; and he used to take what was put in it. But Jesus said, "Let her alone; she has kept this for the day of My burial.

The heart of God touched down in the heart of Mary to show love to Jesus by anointing him for his soon coming death and burial. The Scripture gives us a peek inside to see what was really going on.

Jesus was very close to Martha, Lazarus, and Mary. This was probably the last time they would see him. God moved in Mary's heart for her to show her love to Jesus by putting the costly perfume on his feet and wipe them with her hair. It was a time of intimacy with Jesus and the Father and Mary.

Judas is the thorny vine trying to take the moment captive by putting Mary down and saying that she does not care for the poor. The Scripture allows us to see the real motive of his heart, and Jesus reveals the hidden truth behind her action.

In Mark 14:6–9 (NKJV),

> Jesus said, "Let her alone. Why do you trouble her? **She has done a good work for Me.** For you have the poor with you always, and whenever you wish you may do them good; but Me you do not have always. She has done what she could. She has come beforehand to anoint My body for burial. Assuredly, I say to you, wherever this gospel is preached in the whole world, **what this woman has done will also be told as a memorial to her.**"

Okay, finally back to the parable of the Fig Tree. God has a right to place a demand on us at any given moment for his purpose whenever it pleases him to do so.

> **But you,** when you pray, go into your room, and when you have shut your door, pray to your Father who is in the secret place; and your Father who sees in secret will reward you openly. **(Matthew 6:6 NKJV)**

Declaration of faith: Heavenly Father, I will shut the door to the world and seek you in the secret place of my heart.
What is the nature of God that you see?
God has a tender heart toward his children.
What is the kingdom principle you hear?
Pray with a sincere heart to God, not to impress man.
Enter *Countenance* into search for inquiry.

> Mercy and truth go before Your face. Blessed are the people who know the joyful

sound! **They walk, O Lord, in the light of Your countenance.** (Psalm 89:14–15 NKJV)

> Mary knew the joyful sound of walking in the light of God's countenance. Can't you just see a smile on the face of God when Mary poured the perfume on Jesus's feet and wiped them with her hair? What a tender, loving moment.
>
> We can know that joy also when we walk in the light of mercy and truth and look up to see God smile.

Worship and thanksgiving prayer

God, mercy, and truth go before you. Thank you, O Lord, for the privilege to walk in the light of your countenance and hear the joyful sound of your heart.

Declare truth to receive your treasure:
God, I ask to walk in mercy and truth and that

Our Hearts Be Knit Together in Love

SEEKING HIDDEN TREASURES | 215

The Hiding Place

You are my hiding place; You shall preserve me from trouble; You shall surround me with songs of deliverance. I will instruct you and teach you in the way you should go; I will guide you with My eye.

—Psalm 32:7–8 (NKJV)

Denise and I crisscrossed the land from one side to the other. Then I said, "I want to show you **'the hiding place.'**" Contained in the far-left corner of the property was part of a road from the previous owner. Adjacent to the road was a natural narrow pathway passing through tall yaupon bushes dotted with red berries.

Once again, I explained it looks different now than when my granddaughter and I first discovered it. The first time we reached the end of the path, we walked into a clearing captivated by its beauty. The tall trees were spread apart forming a towering canopy of branches reaching outward to touch one another. The clearing was surrounded by large yaupon bushes. No one could see in from the outside. After the awe of looking at the canopy, there was one more surprise. As our eyes spanned forward, we saw a small lake nestled in the opening with a backdrop of a wooded forest curtain. Because the canopy blocked out the sunshine, there was little undergrowth.

Later I added a three-person swing and a picnic table so I could spend some time there with the grandchildren when they came to visit.

I told Denise that there had been a couple of other landmarks, but the drought a few years ago had changed the landscape. We lost about one-third of our trees.

Declaration of faith: God, you are my hiding place in times of trouble. You guide me in the way I should go.

❖ Is God your hiding place? Where do you go when you are troubled?

What is the nature of God that you see?
God is our hiding place and watches over us to guide us.
What is the kingdom principle you hear?
God will preserve us from trouble by teaching and instructing us in the way we should go.
Enter *Preserve* into search for inquiry.

> *The Lord shall preserve you from all evil; He shall preserve your soul. The Lord shall preserve your going out and your coming in from this time forth, and even forevermore.* (Psalm 121:7–8 NKJV)

> This verse reminds me of a story that our pastor told us about one of his trips. He was sitting next to a woman on the airplane who was very afraid of flying. He told not to worry that he knew the plane was not going down. She asked him how he knew that. He said because "I am on it."
>
> My daughter and granddaughter live in a large city. The people there drive very fast on the freeways, and you had better know what lane to be in before you reach your desired exit. I told Rachael that when I get in the car to come visit, God tells my guardian angel to get up and get ready; Mary is headed to Dallas.
>
> It really is a comfort to know that God preserves our going out and coming in. The eye of God is watching us and watching over us.
>
> The Lord promises to preserve us in the midst of trouble, not that we will be spared

> from trials or tribulation, but he will preserve our soul.

Worship and thanksgiving prayer

God, you are our hiding place. You preserve our soul and our going out and coming in. You deliver us from trouble. Thank you for teaching and instructing us in the way we should go.
Declare truth to receive your treasure:
We will run into you for safety because you preserve us in **the hiding place**.

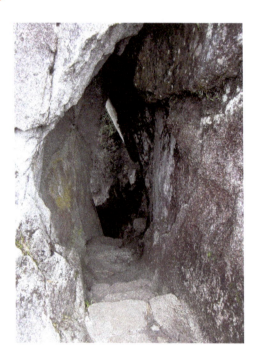

How has your new sight changed your understanding of God?
What do you hear God saying to you?

Journal

The Parable of the Watchman in the Tower

For the Lord said to me, "Go, set a watchman.
Let him declare what he sees.
—Isaiah 21:6 (WEB)

It was time to head back to the house, but there was just one more place I wanted to show Denise. We left through the gate and traveled back down the center lane to another pasture. This was the location of the fawns, Daisy, and her brother. Daisy was still somewhat traumatized by what had happened to her mother, and she stayed in the wooded area of the pasture while we looked around.

Denise, do you remember the parable I told you last week? This is where it took place.

For weeks, I had been cleaning the house of clutter, items that I no longer used, canned food I wasn't going to eat, and giving it away and throwing away anything that didn't work or was broken. Jerry was doing the same process in the barn, but one Saturday, he asked if I would help him. Daisy's pasture backed up to Romeo's pasture. There is no gate between them. Just beyond the fence, there remained remnants of old building materials such as railroad ties used for my tomato garden, wrought iron panels from our previous house, large blocks of stone left over from building our fireplace, etc.

The operation required Jerry to remove a portion of the fence in order to get his tractor in to pick up the heavy items and move them into a more accessible place. It was the season for Romeo to have a full rack of antlers, which could be dangerous if he chose to challenge Jerry. As a precaution, Jerry asked me to **sit in the jeep facing the gap** in the fence with the jeep running while he maneuvered back and forth. It was a hot day, so I located the jeep in the shade under the only tree at the top of the rise of the land at an angle to catch the breeze—in other words, in a strategic position.

After a while, Jerry said that he had a job for me to do. He said, "I think Romeo is hunkered down in the woods because it is too hot. It is safe for you to come in. Would you gather up the smaller debris and put it in the back of the jeep to take it to the dumpster?" Some of the debris was lying in the open and easy to spot; some was entangled in the woods and had to be pulled loose.

While I was sitting in the jeep, God began talking to me. He said, "You are **appointed a watchman in the tower.**" God said, "I will do the heavy lifting, but you are to **stand in the gap for the body of Christ**. It is the gap between 'what we know and what we do.' Be alert to keep them safe from the enemy's tactics."

After I went into Romeo's territory to clean out the remaining debris, God showed me the rest of it. He said we are in a time of "mop up." I knew again what he meant. "Mop up" is a military term used to describe an operation to remove any remaining dangers of an enemy *army* from an area after a victory. In my mind, I saw the danger as a hidden land mine that might blow up in your face to derail your life from completing your purpose in the earth.

Our church, which we call a kingdom community, had a major victory a year ago. In one day, communities in over one hundred nations around the world prayed governmentally, led by a video from Noel Woodroffe, asking God to shake the earth and the heavens.

> *Whose voice shook the earth, then, but now he has promised, saying, "Yet once more I will shake not only the earth, but also the heavens. This phrase, "Yet once more," signifies the removing of those things that are shaken, as of things that have been made, that those things which are not shaken may remain."* (Hebrews 12:26–27 WEB)

Dr. Woodroffe says governmental prayer is the clearest expression of the warfare of the Apostolic Move of God:

> It declares to the principalities and powers of the camp of the enemy the heart of the apostolic impartation in the Church. The apostolic brings to the Church the spiritual position of dominion and rulership manifested forth in executive Kingdom action in the Earth. (Noel Woodroffe, *Governmental Prayer*)

> ***For our wrestling is not against flesh and blood, but against the principalities, against the powers, against the world's rulers of the darkness of this age, and against the spiritual forces of wickedness in the heavenly places***. (Ephesians 6:12 (WEB)

In answer to our prayer, God said,

> *The mighty men of Babylon have forborne to fight, they remain in their strongholds; their might has failed; they are become as women: her dwelling places are set on fire; her bars are broken.* (Jeremiah 51:30 WEB)

Close the gap

Denise and I returned to the house. As she sat relaxing at the table, she said, "I have known an inner quietness before, but I have never felt it like I feel it now."

"Denise, God is saying that he has shown you the lay of the land. You know the time and the season. The ripe fig was a sign that God is placing a demand on your life 'to be' God's purpose in the earth."

It is time to close the gap between what you know and what you do. God is saying for you to lay down "spontaneity" and **put on** "diligence."

Denise shared with me about circumstances in her life. She grew up in a small town of about eight hundred people. Denise's mother died when Denise was only eight years old. Her father remarried and moved into another house with his new bride and two of her children. Denise and her two sisters remained in the house where they had lived with their mother. Daily supervision was provided by her maternal grandmother, who lived next door, her oldest sister, and a company of "nosey" neighbors who were always on the lookout.

Although Denise's teen years were spent with no adults in the house, her father, who was a minister, did set specific guidelines, which he expected to be followed. Because she did not want to be a problem for her dad, she was quiet and compliant. She chose not to date during high school and became active in sports to travel and see a little portion of the world.

When it was time for her to go to college, she chose one far enough from home to give her some space of her own. She did not marry until twenty-one years later. During those years, she developed "a pattern of making decisions in a spontaneous way." She also had learned to "make do" with the circumstances of her environment.

Weeks later, I asked if she had told her husband what I had said.

She replied, "No, I don't think I did."

I asked, "Why not?" If that had been me, I would have gone home and said, "Mary just told me to lay down 'spontaneity' and put on 'diligence.'" What do you think?

Since then, Denise has changed. She now allows her husband to pastor her, collaborates with him to ask for his counsel before she makes important decisions, and she has "put on diligence."

She recently trained for and then completed a bike marathon of 135 miles ridden in two days. This was something she had desired to do for thirty years.

I had asked Denise to assist with the book because of her skill set, her command of the English language, and her ability to ask pertinent questions; but God's ways are higher than our ways. Instead, Denise's life became the teaching dimension, and I became a watchman in the tower.

Declaration of faith: God, shake the things in my life that can be shaken that only the things of you remain.

❖ Do you want God to shake the things in you that are not of him or from him?

What is the nature of God that you see?
God, you are a watchman in the tower warning us of danger.
What is the kingdom principle you hear?
We do not wrestle against flesh and blood but against the principalities, powers, world's rulers of the darkness of this age, and against the spiritual forces of wickedness in the heavenly places.

Enter *Put on* into search for inquiry.

> That you put away, as concerning your former way of life, the old man, that grows corrupt after the lusts of deceit; and that you **be renewed in the spirit of your mind**, and **put on the new man**, who in the likeness of **God has been created in righteousness and holiness of truth**. (Ephesians 4:22–24 WEB)

We are to put away old patterns of thinking. They are like static resisting the voice of God. The danger is that it is very difficult to

> see it because it has become a way of life for us, and we do not even know it. The Word calls it the lust of deceit. We are deceived, but God says to be renewed in the spirit of your mind and put on the new man in the likeness of God.
>
> Be open to hearing and receiving truth.

Worship and thanksgiving prayer

God, you created us in your image of righteousness and holiness of truth. Thank you for renewing the spirit of our mind.

Declare truth to receive your treasure:

I choose to **put on the new man**.

How has your new sight changed your understanding of God?
What do you hear God saying to you?

Journal

A New Heart

A new heart also will I give you, *and a new spirit will I put within you; and I will take away the stony heart out of your flesh, and I will give you a heart of flesh.* ***I will put my Spirit within you****, and cause you to walk in my statutes, and you shall keep my ordinances, and do them.*
—Ezekiel 36:26–27 (WEB)

A new spirit refers to a renewed mind enlightened with understanding in accurate alignment with the will of God. It is a new spirit to actuate your new heart.

I will take away the stony heart that is hard, impenetrable, and cold.

> And I will give you a heart of flesh—One that can feel, and that can enjoy; that can feel love to God and to all men and be a proper habitation for the living God. (Adam Clark's commentary on the Bible)

Late last night, I was feeling achy in my body and agitated enough I could not fall asleep. I contemplated taking some medication but decided to take dominion over my flesh instead.

God reminded me of my last visit to see the grandchildren. They now live out of state, and my grandsons at the time were thirteen years old. One afternoon, one of them had come home, agitated about something that had happened at school which had made him feel bad. It was time to work on homework, and my daughter's attention was required elsewhere, so she asked if I would sit with him and help him to do his timeline. The assignment was to record events on a timeline beginning with your birth and space them out ending with the present day.

The obvious ones are times you have moved to a new home or school with a few special memories in between. I suggested a few, and he was still not able to calm his emotions. I asked myself, "What marked a happy event for him?" He loves to build things with Legos, so I asked him, "What about the time you were given your first Lego kit on your seventh birthday?"

He began to focus on that, and his countenance changed. A week before, he had just returned from a visit with his father to Tennessee to attend a Lego convention, so we added that one also. What we had accomplished was to turn around his focus from himself to something that made him feel good about his life. He was pulling resource from the secret place in his heart and sharing it with me.

I thought I will try that. I asked God to show me a tender moment when he had touched down in my heart on my timeline of walking with him. I thought maybe he would give me dream. I put some lavender oil on my wrists, breathed in the sweet fragrance, and fell right to sleep.

There was no dream. I had a meeting to attend in town about thirty minutes away. A little bit into my journey, I turned on the radio to listen to some music from the sixties. That is a period in my life that holds many good memories for me.

The first song started: **"I've been waiting, I have been waiting so long…"** That hit my spirit with force. Oh, that's me! I began to weep from the depth of my being. I had invited Jesus Christ into my heart at age twelve, and for the last forty years, I had been sharing with God my thoughts and feelings, my hurts and desires, my hopes and fears, my struggles and disappointments which were hidden in my secret place. I shared my love for my Creator, my heavenly Father, and my love for Jesus Christ, my Savior and Redeemer. I had shared my passion to know his heart.

I had found my way back, and God "showed up." I could see his heart of compassion in me! He had knit our hearts together.

God had made a way to return to him where there was no way. Someday I still want to hear that which we all want to hear, which is "Well done, good and faithful servant."

But until that time, I will be content with the voice of Dr. Noel Woodroffe saying, "Now that's a beautiful thing."

The challenge

Watson, is there a gap between what you know and what you do?

Is there a pattern of your former way of life that God is asking you to lay down?

Are you ready and willing to put on the new man?

Talk to God from your secret place, and share the desire of your heart:

1. Ask God to put **a new heart and a new spirit** within you and take away any stony part of your heart that is resisting him. God says he **will put his Spirit within you** and cause you to walk in his ways.
2. Ask God to reveal any old pattern in you that he wants to put away.
3. Ask God what he wants you to "put on." Write them down, and keep these things in prayer.

Ask and keep on asking. Wait for God's timing to see it fulfilled.

Write your answers here:

Well done, Watson!
Now you may collect your reward and move on to the next mountain.

Your reward is to
"Put On"
The Breastplate of Righteousness

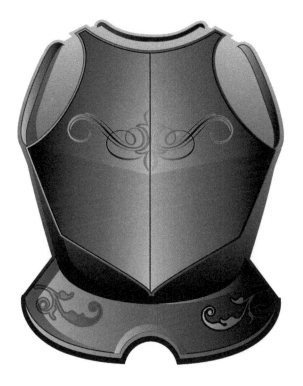

Come along, Watson, don't doddle. Bring your sword of the Spirit, your shield of faith, your helmet of salvation, and we will walk along in peace. I see one more mountain up ahead.

VII

Being

A Dominant Spirit

As the Father has loved me, I also have loved you: ***abide in my love***.
—John 15:9 (DBY)

*Jesus answered him, "**If a man loves me, he will keep my word**. **My Father will love him**, **and** **we will come to him, and make our home with him**.*
—John 14:23 (WEB)

I already mentioned that I live on a farm. Two years ago, my husband built a house for the chickens. It has cement around the bottom so varmints cannot dig under and is surrounded by a chain-link fence on the sides and top. The house itself is wooden and quite sturdy—much better than the previous one. About eight months ago, I had a fright. After dinner one evening, I was being lazy and didn't go to gather the eggs in the chicken coop until about nine. In order to get into the house, I had to step up and over the one-and-a-half-feet-tall opening. The door is about three feet wide and covered with a tight wired mesh. The house has only one breach through a lattice above the door.

With my flashlight in one hand and my egg basket in the other, I went in and gathered the eggs. As I was leaving, I stepped over with my left leg, reached way back to grab the door with my right hand, and saw something in my peripheral vision. I put my light on it with my left hand while still holding on to the door with my right hand. A six-foot snake was slithering along the upper ledge, coiling downward toward my hand. I freaked out! I forcefully projected outward, but my right foot tripped me up, and I landed on my back right hip.

The eggs broke all over my front from my hair to my skirt. I went into the house to find my husband and tell him that I had fallen and hurt myself because of the snake in the house. He grabbed his rifle and went out, but the snake was nowhere to be found. Then he admonished me to never to gather the eggs at night again. I replied, "Don't worry, I won't."

The next day, upon arriving home from work before dark, I went to gather the eggs. I looked through the door, and the six-feet snake was brazenly stretched out straight across the top of the five egg boxes as if he owned the place. He had moved in and taken dominion.

I went back to the house and announced, "He's *baaack*." With his rifle in hand, Jerry went to take a look. Not long after, I heard a loud *Bam*. One shot to the head, and it was history. Jerry lifted it up with the barrel of his gun and dropped it on the grass outside the door. It was still twisting and contorting. I uttered, "That is really creepy." So Jerry went to the nearby jeep, got his machete knife, and with one whack chopped off his head. I said, "Well, that was a good prophetic act."

Unfortunately, that was not the end of the story. Ten days later, on Saturday morning, a man came to visit us to look at the land. When he was just leaving, I walked over to the chicken coop and bent down from my waist to pick up something on the ground. When I had bent down by the coop, it caused the pinching of the sciatic nerve and sent a shooting pain downward all the way to my foot. I was barely able to walk the ten feet to the gravel road in front of our house. Thankfully, I made it to lie down.

I signaled Jerry to come over and told him, "I cannot walk. You will have to get the car, lift me into it (which was no small task), and drive me to the emergency room." While riding in the car, I was okay, but to move was excruciatingly painful. The doctor gave me IV pain medication. Eleven hours later at 3:00 a.m., I was moved to a room. I lay on my left side for four days. The doctor informed me that he couldn't do anything more for me, so I would have to leave.

The hospital did send me home with a walker that had a seat so I could use it like a wheelchair. It took six weeks of pain medication and an injection in my spine before I could walk even a short distance.

On the Friday before this incident, I had purchased an airplane ticket to attend my twin grandsons' graduation ceremony from sixth grade. The boys had worked so hard in school, diligently attending tutorials one and a half hours after school four days every week for six years. I really, really wanted to be there to congratulate them with my grandmotherly affirmation of "Well done, guys!"

Healing was very slow. I had one hour of home nurse care three times a week along with some physical therapy, and my husband helped me on the weekends. Monday before my scheduled Wednesday flight to see my grandsons, I was still weak from the medication and being in bed so long, but I tried to go outside to weed a little bit in my garden.

I believed God was telling me to go, but I was too exhausted to even pack, much less fly two legs to Ohio. After fifteen minutes of weed pulling, I sighed to myself, "There is no way I will be able to do this."

Our pastor had just been teaching us about pulling down resource from the upper realm into the earthly realm. We had been taught to say, **"What is impossible here is possible there"**—meaning nothing is impossible for God. So I just said it out loud while standing on my porch. Instantly I was energized. I had energy to pack and get ready. I called the airlines to order wheelchairs to take me through the airport's security and to make my connections for the flights. In Dallas I had a two-hour layover. At that time, I was only able to walk about thirty feet. An attendant wheeled me through the airport onto the tram and to the gate area. When we arrived, I could hardly believe the goodness of God. Within a thirty-foot radius was a fast-food restaurant where I could get lunch and a bag of ice to put in my cold pack for my hip. There was a large room with padded lounge chairs that extended outward so I could put up my feet and outlets to charge my electronic devices. On the other side was a restroom, and around the corner was my gate!

The graduation was really special. It began with a wide-screen presentation called "Then and Now" displaying a baby picture and a present-day picture of each student in alphabetical order. It was followed by a presentation called "Twins and Now," which showed six pairs of twins including my grandsons. Each slide showed the twins as toddlers in an activity followed by a present-day picture with the twins in the exact same pose. It was very clever. The next day, all the sixth graders had a day of fun activities in the park, which just happened to be across the street from my daughter's house. Once again I was able to walk there. God is so faithful!

Keep the Door Shut

For God didn't give us a spirit of fear, but of
power, love, and self-control.
—2 Timothy 1:7 (WEB)

Ever since the snake incident, my husband has been collecting the eggs because I have not felt comfortable doing it. Last week, I decided I just needed to get over it, so I went in to gather the eggs and remembered the Scripture about God giving us dominion in the garden of Eden. I also thought about something my former Bible teacher of many years ago said that she had done. Mrs. Hromas told us about her going camping and finding out that there were mosquitos, so she walked off a space around her tent and forbade the mosquitos to enter that area in the name of Jesus. I am not sure how it worked for her, but I remembered the story, and that is exactly what I did. I forbid snakes to enter the house.

I told my husband about what I had done, and he said, "You will still have snakes."

"Hmmm. Really?"

"Yes, the only way to not have snakes is to **keep the door shut**."

During the day, we leave the door to the chicken house open so the chickens can enter the fenced pasture to free range, and at night we close the door to keep them safe.

Ohhh! The light went on. I understood that the door is the door to my mind. The only way to keep thoughts from the enemy from taking dominion in my mind was to keep the door shut by taking every thought captive.

Also keep the door shut by not reading books, not listening to music, not watching movies or television, not playing games that entertain "vain imaginations" from the enemy.

> *Don't turn aside; for [then would you go] after vain things which can't profit nor deliver, for they are vain.* (1 Samuel 12:21)

I was not injured from the snake. Rather, I was injured because of my "fear" of the snake. Fear is NEVER from God. Because of the fear, I suffered injury, pain, and torment.

> *There is no fear in love, but perfect love casts out fear; for fear has torment, and he that fears has not been made perfect in love.* (1 John 4:18 DBY)

Second Timothy 1:7 states that **God has given us a spirit of power, love, and self-control**. Fear is a choice. If a man has perfect love toward God, he has no dread of the future or fear beyond the grave. God delivers us through his love for us. Love and fear are opposites. Love cannot be found in fear, and fear cannot exist in perfect love.

Several years ago, Dr. Woodroffe was teaching about the sovereignty of God, and a vortex appeared in the sky above the building where he was speaking.

He called it a "prophetic expression."

The image describes two levels of sight. The top of The Vortex points to a position of limited sight, confusion and fear. The bottom of The Vortex shows the movement to peace, understanding and faith. (DNW)

In the top part of The Vortex, there is no discernable pattern. This part of The Vortex can be described with words like arbitrary… chaos…disorder…disconnectedness. In the bottom part of The Vortex, as it narrows, things resolve into a state of greater order, to a point of resolution. (DNW)

The Vortex describes the process of a **"dominant spirit"** moving from darkness resolving itself into truth. The top part represents one who has no sight of the kingdom; they cannot see beyond the disorder and darkness. The bottom part represents the believer moving to sight, to peace, to understanding, and to faith. The movement toward light is the process of "laying down and putting on." You are laying down your flesh and putting on Christ. **It is the power to put on Christ and the self-control to make right choices.**

Declaration of faith: God, I pray to have a dominant spirit of power, love, and self-control.

❖ Do you want to walk in the perfect love of God and overcome fear?

What is the nature of God that you see?
God is perfect love.
What is the kingdom principle you hear?
Do not think on vain things that cannot profit or deliver. Think on the Love of God for you and me. We love him because he loved us first.

Enter *love* into search for inquiry.

> *I hate the double-minded, but I **love** Your law. You are my hiding place and my shield; I hope in Your word.* (Psalm 119:113–114 NKJV)
>
> *Count it all joy, my brothers, when you fall into various temptations, **knowing that the testing of your faith produces endurance**. Let endurance have its perfect work, that you may be perfect and complete, lacking in nothing. But if any of you lacks wisdom, let him ask of God, who gives to all liberally and without reproach; and it will be given to him. But let him ask in faith, without any doubting, for **he who doubts is like a wave of the sea**, **driven by the wind and tossed**. For let that man not think that he will receive anything from the Lord. **He is a double-minded man, unstable in all his ways**.* (James 1:2–8 WEB)
>
> Fear and love are not compatible. To have both is to be double-minded and unstable.
>
> Take note that when it says God has given us a spirit of power, love, and self-control, <u>power comes first</u>.

We love Him, because he first loved us. (1 John 4:19 WEB)

Worship and thanksgiving prayer

God, you are a God of perfect love. Thank you that you first loved us. Thank you that you give us the power to walk in that love and not be double-minded.

Declare truth to receive your treasure:
I desire to have a spirit of power, love, and

How has your new sight changed your understanding of God?
What do you hear God saying to you?

Journal

The Groan

For most assuredly in this <u>we groan</u>, longing to be clothed with our habitation which is from heaven.
—2 Corinthians 5:2 (WEB)

Put on the new man, *that is being renewed in knowledge after the image of his Creator.*
—Colossians 3:10 (WEB)

Put on…*a heart of compassion, kindness, lowliness, humility, and perseverance.*
—Colossians 3:12 (WEB)

But above all these things **put on love**, *which is the* **bond of perfection**. *And let the* **peace of God rule in your hearts**, *to which also* **you were called in one body**; *and be thankful.*
—Colossians 3:14–15 NKJV

Watson, remember at the beginning I told you that God said to me to put on compassion, and I asked him how do I do that? He said write a book. This book represents a groan to be clothed with compassion.

But **put on the Lord Jesus Christ**, and make no provision for the flesh, for its lusts. (Romans 13:14 WEB)

Declaration of faith: I put on the Lord Jesus Christ and make no provision for the flesh, for its lusts.

- ❖ Is there a groan in you for more of Christ?
- ❖ If you were to put on compassion, how would compassion look in you?
- ❖ Ask God to show you.

What is the nature of God that you see?

In God and Jesus Christ is the bond of perfection which is love. Jesus demonstrated **a heart of compassion, kindness, lowliness, humility, and perseverance**.

What is the kingdom principle you hear?

Put on the new man by being renewed in the knowledge of our Creator. Long to be clothed with a habitation from heaven.

Enter *dwelling* into search for inquiry.

> ***Till Your people pass over***, *O Lord, till the people pass over Whom You have purchased.* (Exodus 15:16–18 NKJV)

*You will bring them in and plant them in the mountain of your inheritance, in the place, O Lord, which you have made for your own **dwelling**, the sanctuary, O Lord, which your hands have established. "The Lord shall reign forever and ever."*

> We have been purchased by the blood of Jesus Christ to be his inheritance and the dwelling place of his glory—a place where the Lord shall reign forever and ever.
>
> Our inheritance is to be clothed with a habitation from heaven.
>
> When we pass over from this realm into the heavenly realm, it says that we will **dwell** in the sanctuary of the Lord which he has established.
>
> For indeed we who are in this tent do groan, being burdened; not that we desire to be unclothed, but that **we desire to be**

> **clothed, that what is mortal may be swallowed up by life.** (2 Corinthians 5:4 WEB)
>
> Our desire is that the mortal be overtaken by the immortal. There will be a time, a generation when this will happen. We shall dwell in the sanctuary of the Lord.

Worship and thanksgiving prayer

God, you are the peace that dwells in our heart. It is your persevering love that calls us to dwell in one body, the body of Christ. Thank you for the love that bonds us together as one, with one heart and one mind.

Declare truth to receive your treasure:

I groan to be

Clothed with a Habitation from Heaven

How has your new sight changed your understanding of God?
What do you hear God saying to you?

Journal

Designing a New Humanity

For the Kingdom of God is not in word, but in **power**.
—1 Corinthians 4:20 (WEB)

If you were to look at a newly made wooden chair, you might say to the carpenter, "I like your new creation." That would be in error. It's a new design. The person did not create the wood. What about plastic? He or she didn't create the chemical elements.

All creation came out of God to be displayed in the earth. What about new designs? Those come from the mind of God also. Your personal design is expressed in your choices, which are a manifestation of your personality.

Last week I went into the kitchen to prepare myself some lunch. In one of my usual conversations with God, I was telling him that I wanted to eat something different from my customary sliced chicken with melted cheese on top. God explained that it is not the food you choose but the way you put it together that makes it different.

If you combine several foods together seasoned with spices and assembled in an artistic way, you might be called a chef. If you cross-pollinate to design a new rose, you might give it a name and call it your new creation, but you did not create the original roses from which it came.

Design and creation are two totally different things; however, both originate in the mind of God. God created the heavens and the earth out of nothing that existed. He designed man from the dust of the earth which he had already created. Then God breathed life into man.

> *Yahweh* **God formed man from the dust of the ground, and breathed into his nostrils the breath of life; and man became a living soul**. (Genesis 2:7 WEB)

SEEKING HIDDEN TREASURES

> The breath of God is the power to exist.

> Let every soul be in subjection to the higher authorities, for **there is no authority except from God**, and **those who exist are ordained by God**. (Romans 13:1 WEB)

> From now on, **the Son of Man will be seated at the right hand of the power of God**. (Luke 22:69 WEB)

> Behold, I send forth the promise of my Father on you. But wait in the city of Jerusalem until you are **clothed with power from on high**. (Luke 24:49 WEB)

> But **you will receive power** when the Holy Spirit has come upon you. (Acts 1:8 WEB)

> That he would grant you, according to the riches of his glory, that you may be **strengthened with power through his Spirit in the inward man**. (Ephesians 3:16 WEB)

God strengthens us with power through the Holy Spirit to exist in the likeness of Christ in our inward man.

> God said, "Let us make man in our image, after our likeness…" God created man in his own image. In God's image he created him; male and female he created them. (Genesis 1:26–27 WEB)

Declaration of faith: God, strengthen my inward man with power to become disentangled from everything in this

world that stands in opposition to your original design for me.

❖ Do you want God's design for your life?

What is the nature of God that you see?
God is the highest authority of life. There is no authority except from God, and those who exist are ordained by God.

What is the kingdom principle you hear?
We are dust. It is only the power of God that gives us life, shapes that life, and defines that life within us. I submit my soul to his authority.

Enter *Power* into search for inquiry.

> *But indeed **for this purpose I have raised you up, that I may show My power in you, and that My name may be declared in all the earth.*** (Exodus 9:16 NKJV)

> *He changes the times and the seasons; he removes kings, and sets up kings; he gives wisdom to the wise, and knowledge to those who have understanding;* **he reveals the deep and secret things;** *he knows what is in the darkness, and the light dwells with him.* (Daniel 2:21–22 WEB)
>
> This scripture speaks about the authority of God in the earth. He controls the times and the seasons. He raises up whom he chooses for his purpose and reveals the deep and secret things at his discretion.

Worship and thanksgiving prayer

God, the power of your breath is life to us. Thank you that you raise us up by your power to declare your name in all the earth.

Declare truth to receive your treasure:

I desire to have the

Humility of Being Dust

How has your new sight changed your understanding of God?
What do you hear God saying to you?

Journal

Building a Kingdom Civilization

I saw an angel flying in mid heaven, **having an eternal Good News to proclaim to those who dwell on the earth,** *and to every nation, tribe, language, and people. He said with a loud voice, "Fear the Lord, and give him glory; for the hour of his judgment has come.* Worship him who made the heaven, the earth, the sea, and the springs of waters. *Another, a second angel, followed, saying,* **"Babylon the great has fallen."**
—Revelation 14:6–8

Revelation 14 speaks of a fallen world system—Babylon. We are presently in a time when one civilization is breaking down and another is being built up.

The angel has flown, and we can see the Babylonian system in the earth falling before our eyes as more and more corruption is being exposed. Political, economic, and false relational structures are breaking down.

The earth is groaning in floods, fires, earthquakes, and rampant devastation; however, when the darkness gets darker, the light becomes brighter.

In this tumultuous time, God is revealing himself as never before. He is looking for vessels in which to pour himself. This is beautifully illustrated in Jeremiah 18:1–6. Jeremiah was instructed to go down to the potter's house and see what the potter was doing. He was making something on the wheel.

> *But the vessel that he was making of clay was spoiled in the hand of the potter; so he remade it into another vessel, as it pleased the potter to make.*

God is the potter, and he wants to form and shape a people for his purposes. In addition, he wants to build a kingdom civilization. Again, we look to the prophet Jeremiah as he writes:

> *At what instant I shall speak concerning a nation, and concerning a kingdom, to* **pluck up and to break down and to destroy it**. (Jeremiah 18:7 WEB)

> *At what instant I shall speak concerning a nation, and concerning a kingdom, to* **build and to plant it**. (Jeremiah 18:9 WEB)

Remember my friend Karla who identified my war cry. She moved back to Trinidad several years ago. Even though Karla and I lived in different cities, rarely saw each other, and did not talk often, I was attracted to her. She invited me to visit with her and her family just before she left. As I was driving to her home, I began to weep, thinking I would really miss her when she moved. Amid my sobs, I asked God, "What is it about Karla that I love so much? He uttered, "She is **precision clothed in humility**."

God is not looking for perfection. Jeremiah 31:32 says that God is making a covenant to put his ways within us and write it on our heart and he will be our God and we shall be his people. God has created a new thing in the earth—people whose hearts are like his heart.

> **Jesus said, "I will build my church, and the gates of hell shall not prevail against it."** (Matthew 16:18 KJV)

And that is you and me.

Declaration of faith: God, you are the potter, and I am the clay. Make me into a vessel pleasing to you. Pluck up and tear down in me so you can build and plant your ways in me.

Make me into a new vessel that is fit for your purpose and one that you can pour yourself into.

> ❖ Do you want God to make you into a new vessel pleasing to him?

What is the nature of God that you see?
God is the Creator of heaven and earth and is a builder and designer of man.

What is the kingdom principle you hear?
God will pluck up, tear down, and destroy a civilization in order to build and plant a new civilization. Jesus said, "I will build my church."

Enter *Build* **into search for inquiry.**

> And whoever does not bear his cross and come after Me cannot be My disciple. For which of you, **intending to** *build* a tower, **does not sit down first and count the cost, whether he has enough to finish it**—lest, after he has laid the foundation, and is not able to finish. (Luke 14:27–29 NKJV)

The apostle Paul gives us the keys to spiritual maturity in Philippians 3:7–14:

1. **Calculate loss** (vv. 7–8) *I once thought these things were valuable, but* **now I consider them worthless** *because of what Christ has done. Yes, everything else is worthless* **when compared with the infinite value of knowing Christ Jesus** *my Lord. For His sake I have discarded every-*

> *thing else, counting it all as garbage, so that I could gain Christ.*
> 2. **Redefine your starting context** (v. 9) *And **be found in Him**, not having a righteousness that comes from God and is by faith.*
> 3. **Conform to his death** (v. 10) *That I may know him and the power of his resurrection, and the fellowship of his sufferings, **being conformed to his death**.*
> 4. **Strain heavenward** (vv. 13–14) *But one thing I do: forgetting what is behind and straining towards what is ahead, **I press on** towards the goal to win the prize for which **God has called me heavenwards in Christ Jesus**.*
>
> Resurrected life in Christ is raised up from the ashes of sacrifice and death. Not our will but God's will be done in us.

Worship and thanksgiving prayer

God, we worship you, for you have made the heaven, the earth, the sea, and the springs of waters. Thank you for forming us into a new vessel fit for your use and your presence. We strain heavenward and press on to the goal to win the prize for which you have called us.

Declare truth to receive your treasure:

My desire is to have

Functional Oneness

(To function in the earth in oneness with God—
in motive, will, actions, and obedience.)

How has your new sight changed your understanding of God?
What do you hear God saying to you?

Journal

Overcoming

I have told you these things, that in me you may have peace. In the world you have oppression; but cheer up! I have overcome the world.
—John 16:33 (WEB)

Jesus was talking to his disciples to prepare them for his departure just prior to his arrest. He was warning them to expect trouble and tribulation beyond their control after he was gone. He instructed, "Take courage" **in me so that you may have peace**.

My daughter just called, asking for counsel to overcome a situation which had occurred a couple of years ago. Her family was invited to a Fourth of July celebration which included a gathering of extended family members and friends. She was somewhat concerned about attending because it was loosely supervised, and she did not know some of the people participating; however, she went anyway.

At dark they set up lawn chairs in a horseshoe formation around a makeshift firepit where the kids were playing with sparklers. As the evening progressed, two young men were goofing off, indifferent to the potential danger of fireworks. As "boys will be boys," they had decided they would surprise the crowd by lighting a Roman candle with ten balls shooting upward into the sky. One of my grandsons was sitting in a wobbly camp chair and was feeling unstable, so my daughter exchanged seats with him. Two minutes later, one of the young men lit the fuse and clumsily knocked over the Roman candle. The balls shot out with force, hitting my daughter in the chest and shoulder area. She began screaming. Her shirt was in flames, and her husband rushed over to tear the shirt from her body. She was badly burned and has scars to this day.

She received an apology for the incident, but no offer was made to help pay for her medical expenses or a maid to clean her house while she was healing.

She was calling because she did not have peace. Scheduled to have a serious surgery to have a cyst removed from her spine, she was concerned because a couple of the people involved in the fireworks incident were coming to her house shortly after the surgery to help her husband with household chores and staying through the holidays.

I told you that I do understand trauma to the body because of being hit by the car when I was young. It does stay with you in your memory and emotions for a long time. I told her to first separate the trauma from the uncompassionate people who caused it. The two were entangled together. Next, let's deal with the trauma. The trauma is real. So how do you overcome it to have peace?

Bad things do happen over which we have no control. Jesus gave us a promise that he has overcome the world so in him we <u>may</u> have peace. It is a choice. You may ask, "Where was Jesus in the midst of this situation?" I reminded her that God made her a promise to make a way where there was no way for the boys. If you had not exchanged seats with your ten-year-old son, the trajectory of the balls would have hit him in the face, possibly blinding him and certainly traumatizing him and burning his face. I explained to her that that is when you offer up the sacrifice of praise with a grateful heart to thank God for his goodness and mercy. She agreed that she could easily do that, but what about the other? I responded that when you have disentangled the two, then I believe you will heal from the trauma and can see the other in a diffident light; then you can ask God for wisdom to address the present-day situation.

> *For I know the thoughts that I think toward you, says the Lord,* **thoughts of peace** *and not of evil,* *to give you a future and a hope.* *Then*

*you will **call upon Me and go and pray to Me, and I will listen to you**. And you **will seek Me and find Me, when you search for Me with all your heart**. **I will be found by you, says the Lord**.* (Jeremiah 29:11–14 NKJV)

Declaration of faith: God, I will seek you and search for you with all my heart. I will call upon you and pray to you, for you are my hope of a future of peace.

❖ Do you want a future of hope and peace?

What is the nature of God that you see?
Jesus has overcome the world and is our peace. He wants to be found in us and have communion with us.
What is the kingdom principle you hear?
If you search for God with your whole heart, call upon him, and pray to him, he will listen and give you peace and a hope of a future in him.
Enter *Peace* into search for inquiry.

*As for me, I will call upon God, And the Lord shall save me. Evening and morning and at noon I will pray, and cry aloud, And He shall hear my voice. He has **redeemed my soul in peace** **from the battle** that was against me.* (Psalm 55:16–18 NKJV)

Redemption is peace with God and the peace of God within us. Isn't that the battleground of our soul? We long for it, we yearn for it, we pray for it, and we hope for it.

I watched a biography tonight of a very famous author who lived over a hundred years

> ago and was honored all around the world for his books and speaking tours. He had a loving family, attained wealth and admiration; but in the process of seeking even more money, he let it all slip through his fingers. Toward the end of his life, he became depressed and bitter toward God.
>
> It made me think about my life, and I said to God, "I want to finish well with peace in my soul and thanksgiving on my lips." How do you want to finish your journey?

Worship and thanksgiving prayer

God, you are the God of peace and hope. Thank you that I can call on you morning, noon, and night, and you are always there. You hear my voice and give me hope for the future.

Declare truth to receive your treasure:

God, you are the

Peace in My Soul

How has your new sight changed your understanding of God?

What do you hear God saying to you?

Journal

Hope Anchors Our Soul

*It is **impossible for God to lie**, we may have a strong encouragement, who have fled for **refuge** to take hold of the **hope set before us**. This **hope we have as an anchor of the soul, a hope both sure and steadfast**.*
—Hebrews 6:18–19 (WEB)

> **"It is the power of the journey that has forged us and made us strong."**

Forging is a manufacturing process involving the shaping of metal using localized compressive forces. The blows are delivered with a hammer. Forging can produce a piece that is stronger than an equivalent cast or machined part. As the metal is shaped during the forging process, its internal grain texture deforms to follow the general shape of the part. As a result, the texture variation is continuous throughout the part, giving rise to a piece with improved strength characteristics. (Wikipedia)

Forging is a lengthy process designed to strengthen our resolve, steadfastness, dedication, and faithfulness to be shaped by the hand of God (not cast by the culture or machined by the media). It is the molding of our heart to be transformed and conformed to be a replica of the heart of Jesus Christ.

Forging is a process of letting go of earthly values and apprehending godly values and walking it out through our daily choices.

You don't know how to exist (your whole structure of being) until you read the Word of God.

- How to think

- How to feel
- How to posture yourself
- How to build a set of priorities in your life

We live in an environment where Babylon (systems of the world) will try and pull us into its shape. We live in time, but we receive wisdom and direction from the eternal dimension that tells us how to think and act accurately.

Until you read the Word of God, you don't know how to be, how to calibrate your insides, what you are called to be, or how to move. You will be pushed and pulled by the influences of your flesh, by desires and timings that come from Babylon.

We set our heart on a course to please God.

> *For indeed we who are in this tent do groan, being burdened; not that we desire to be unclothed, but that we desire to be clothed, that what is mortal may be swallowed up by life. Now he who made us for this very thing is God, who also gave to us the down payment of the Spirit. Therefore, we are always confident and know that while we are at home in the body, we are absent from the Lord;* **for we walk by faith, not by sight**. *We are of good courage, I say, and are willing rather to be absent from the body, and to be at home with the Lord. Therefore also* **we make it our aim**, *whether at home or absent,* **to be well pleasing to him**. (2 Corinthians 5:4–9 WEB)

Faith keeps us alive, keeps us in hope, and keeps us rising up / lifting up a standard in the darkness of the day. **We live by believing, not by sight.**

Declaration of faith: God, I make it my aim to be pleasing to you and to walk by faith not by sight.

❖   Do you want to be pleasing to God?

What is the nature of God that you see?
It is impossible for God to lie. He is our refuge and a steadfast hope of an encourager of the future.

What is the kingdom principle you hear?
Walk by faith not by sight. Hope is the anchor of our soul.
Enter *hope* into search for inquiry.

> *Being therefore justified by faith, we have peace with God through our Lord Jesus Christ; through whom we also have our access by faith into this grace in which we stand.* ***We rejoice in hope of the glory of God****. Not only this, but we also rejoice in our sufferings, knowing that suffering works perseverance; and perseverance, proven character; and proven character, hope:* and ***hope doesn't disappoint us, because God's love has been poured out into our hearts through the Holy Spirit who was given to us***. (Romans 5:1–5 WEB)

> In these verses, we can see the journey from faith to peace to grace to hope to suffering to perseverance to proven character to hope that does not disappoint to God's love poured out in our hearts and the Holy Spirit given to us.
>
> We rejoice in hope of the glory of God. Glory is seen in God's character and attributes of brightness, splendor, magnificence, maj-

> esty. God's glory is also the external manifestation of his being. We give God praise and honor to his glory and majesty.
>
> Our hope is to see those attributes of his character manifested in us poured out into our hearts by his love.

Worship and thanksgiving prayer

God, we honor you and praise your glory. Thank you that you are a God that cannot lie. Thank you for a journey of the hope of seeing your character manifested in us.

Declare truth to receive your treasure:

Hope to Anchor My Soul

How has your new sight changed your understanding of God?

What do you hear God saying to you?

Journal

The Heart Follows the Treasure

*But **lay up for yourselves treasures in heaven**, where neither moth nor rust consume, and where thieves don't break through and steal; for **where your treasure is, there your heart will be also**.*
—Matthew 6:20–21 (WEB)

If God be the treasure of our souls, our hearts (i.e., our affections and desires) will be placed on things above.

> Man may try to persuade himself that he will have a treasure on earth and a treasure in heaven also, but in the long-run, one or the other will assert its claim to be *the* treasure, and will claim the no longer divided allegiance of the heart. (*Elliott's Bible Commentary*)

One day while Jesus was speaking to the multitudes, his mother and brothers were seeking to speak to him but were unable to get to him because of the crowd.

When Jesus was informed that his mother, brothers, and sisters were outside, looking for him,

> *He answered them, "Who are my mother and my brothers?" Looking around at those who sat around him, he said, "Behold, my mother and my brothers! **For whoever does the will of God, the same is my brother, and my sister, and mother**."* (Mark 3:33–35 WEB)

One day last week, I felt a grieving throughout the day. My sister and I had been trying to coordinate a family reunion. Things began falling apart as family members had issues that prevented them from hosting it at their house, so we were left without a venue.

But in the prior weeks, I had been going through family pictures to select some to put in an album for the reunion. God began dealing with me about my roots, which extended deep into my past and how I was holding on to some of the good times to define me.

Then God began sifting through them one by one like sifting sand. They were temporary pleasures, smoke and mirrors with no lasting value to define me, and my thoughts shifted from the temporary to the eternal.

In dealing with my family, whom I love very much, I realized that my church community is my true family. These are people with whom I journey within the purposes of God for my life and his purpose in the earth. This is an eternal bond joined by the Holy Spirit. It is a forever family. This is a family that allows me to be my authentic self and helps me to grow in the ways of the Lord. This is a family that encourages me to journey on through the storms. This is a family that prays for each other. This is a family with whom I can share my deepest desires, and they understand the context from which I speak.

The apostle Paul said,

> <u>I consider everything a loss</u> because of the surpassing worth of knowing Christ Jesus, my Lord, for whose sake I have lost all things. I consider them garbage, that I may gain Christ and be found in Him. (Philippians 3:8–9 NIV)

Mortality has temporary joys, but it all passes away. We cannot hold onto things from the past to boost our confidence. The only true confidence is being in the likeness of Christ. Anything of the earth is not eternal and is garbage in the eyes of God. The real you is God in you, not the mortal and temporary joys which can serve as a way to get you through hard times. Our confidence has to be in God—this is sustainable, this is eternal, this is true reality. Nothing in this physical world is truly real. It is a facade. The world system must not be allowed to imprint us or allow any circumstances in our life to shape our identity, whether they are blessings or disasters. We only allow ourselves to be defined by God.

> *Therefore let us also, seeing we are surrounded by so great a cloud of witnesses, lay aside every weight and the sin which so easily entangles us, and let us run with patience the race that is set before us, looking to Jesus, the author and perfecter of faith, who* **for the joy that was set before him endured the cross**, *despising shame, and has sat down at the right hand of the throne of God.* (Hebrews 12:1–2 WEB)

Joy is a necessity in life. It motivates us to press on; it provides tenacity and strength for completion, and like hope, it is an anchor/stabilizer for our soul (mind, will, emotions).

Declaration of faith:

> *Bless the LORD, O my soul: and all that is within me, bless his holy name.* (Psalm 103:1 KJV)

❖ **Watson, do you want to lay up treasures in heaven?**

Let's take a look to see what is in your treasure chest

A Mind Set on Things Above, Increased Faith to Be Pleasing to God, A Pure Heart to See God, Knowledge of True Identity, Trust in God, Set Free to Abide in Truth, Receive Wisdom and Get Understanding, Discernment to Know God's Plan and Purpose, An Abundance of Grace, Wisdom to Build Accurately, A Hearing Heart to Understand God's Ways

Power to Begin Anew, Filled with the Holy Spirit, Fear of the Lord, Sufficient Grace, Walk in Love, A Light for My Path, A Grateful Heart

Compassion to Learn God's Ways, Strength in My Core, The Door of Hope, Song of Praise, The Battle is the Lord's, Taking Thoughts Captive, Endurance to Persevere to the Finish, Know the Mystery of the Kingdom of God, Power of His Might, The Key of David

> Go with Grace, Our Hearts Knit Together in Love, The Hiding Place, Put on the New Man
>
> A Spirit of Power, Love and Self-Control, Clothed with a Habitation from Heaven, Humility of Being Dust, Functional Oneness, Peace in My Soul, Hope to Anchor My Soul

For this day is holy to our Lord. Do not sorrow, **for the joy of the Lord is your strength**. (Nehemiah 8:10 NKJV)

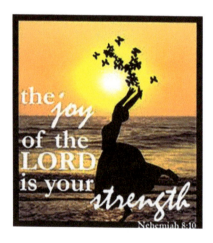

Stand up, and bless the Lord your God forever and ever!
Blessed be your glorious name, which is exalted above all blessing and praise!
You alone are the Lord; you have made heaven, The heaven of heavens, with all their host,

The earth and everything on it, the seas and
 all that is in them,
And you preserve them all. The host of heaven
 worships you.
(Nehemiah 9:5–6 NKJV)

Well, done Watson!

Gird your waist with truth!

I just heard the news that God is assembling his army to be synchronized and integrated into oneness expressing true kingdom life in Christ.

Put on your breastplate of righteousness, shod your feet with the preparation of the gospel of peace, take the shield of faith with which you will be able to quench all the fiery darts of the wicked one, put on your helmet of salvation, and bring the sword of the Spirit along with all your treasures of wisdom and knowledge. Are you ready?

If you would like to be assembled with the mighty army of God, please sign your name on the line below.

Name_____

Date_____

Love for the Body of Christ

*And He Himself gave some to be apostles, some prophets, some evangelists, and some pastors and teachers, for the equipping of the saints for the work of ministry, for the **edifying of the body of Christ**, till we all come to the unity of the faith and of the knowledge of the Son of God, to a perfect man, **to the measure of the stature of the fullness of Christ**.*
—Ephesians 4:11–13 NKJV

Biblical love is not an earthly emotional state of being. Love is a powerful overriding spiritual principle that is the foundation of all relevant spiritual life and activity in earth, and it forms the basis for life in eternity.

> *But now faith, hope, and love remain— these three. The greatest of these is love.* (1 Corinthians 13:13 WEB)

God tells us that faith, hope, and love will last forever. These are eternal treasures, but God says the greatest is love. Biblical love is birthed from the spirit of a person. It is not of the flesh, emotions, or the soul. It is not a feeling.

Loves begins in the spirit and, therefore, love for the body of Christ is a revelation position. You cannot love the body of Christ without some level of spiritual understanding.

We are not required by God to love Christianity. The structure of the religion called Christianity is a different structure from the entity that is called **the body of Christ**.

> *Upon this rock I will build my church; and the gates of Hades shall not prevail against it.* (Matthew 16:18 ASV)

Christ says he will build his church, and anything built by Jesus, we have the capacity to love. He will build his church. It will be full of dominion and power.

> *And he is the head of the body, the church.*
> *(Colossians 1:18 ASV)*

Relationship between Jesus and the body of Christ

The head is connected to the body, which is an intimate connection. In Ephesians 5, Paul says the husband is the head of the wife as Christ is the head of the church's body. The wife is to submit to her husband just as we, the body of Christ, submit to the head, which is Christ.

Paul goes on to say for husbands to love their wives just as Christ loved the church and gave himself up for her. Who hates his own body?

> *After all, no one ever hated his own body, but he feeds and cares for it just as Christ feeds and cares for the church. (v. 29)*

> *And He wants to present Her to himself as a radiant church, a shining church, without stain, without wrinkle, without any blemish. (v. 27)*

To love the church is to love yourself. **So when we talk about loving the body of Christ, we are talking about loving ourselves.** Also the body is not separate from the head. The two are intricately and intimately connected. The church is indivisible from Christ. The bond cannot be broken, **so to love the body of Christ is to love Christ himself.**

So, what is love? Love is

- **deep identification with Christ and with his body,**

- **faith-filled support for Christ and for his body,**
- **the desire to share what we have with saints of the body of Christ,**
- **the determination that all must inherit equally,**
- **responsibility carried by those who have been blessed beyond measure.**

Watson, I have one last clue for you:
What was on the heart of Jesus when he prayed to the Father for his disciples in his final hours? (John 17)

> <u>**Sanctify them in your truth**</u>. Your word is truth. (John 17:17 WEB)

> I in them, and you in me, that they may be <u>**perfected into one**</u>; that the world may know that you sent me, and <u>**loved them, even as you loved me.**</u> (John 17:23 WEB)

> Father, I desire that they also whom you have given me <u>**be with me where I am**</u>, that they may see my glory, which you have given me, for you loved me before the foundation of the world. (John 17:24 WEB)

Back to where? Back to God's original plan for his creation.
Declaration of truth: God, I love you because you first loved me.
Watson, receive your greatest treasure!

God's Eternal Love

Pay It Forward

If this book has blessed you, would you pray about buying one or two copies and giving the book to a friend? I pray this book has been an encouragement to you in your life's journey and partnership with God. Let us encourage one another.

> In the day that I called, you answered me. You encouraged me with strength in my soul.
> —Psalm 138:3 WEB

About the Author

Mary R. Sumners is a member of Genesis Centre, a kingdom community based in Dallas, Texas.

A couple of years ago, Mary was challenged by her sixteen-year-old granddaughter to explore and investigate the meaning of a prophetic word given to her by her camp counselor: "You will move mountains." She asked her grandmother, "What does it mean to move mountains?" This small request opened the door of investigation and illumination as Mary realized the danger of losing this present-day generation to ever-increasing darkness and deception. Mary shares her personal forty-year journey into increasing maturity by learning how to strengthen core values, guard the heart, and armor the mind.

Mary resides in Texas, with her husband. She has two daughters and four grandchildren

Printed in the USA
CPSIA information can be obtained
at www.ICGtesting.com
LVHW051154211123
764186LV00007B/10